Cotswold Village School

from Victorian Times

MICHAEL BOYES

PUBLISHED BY
THE RISSINGTONS LOCAL HISTORY SOCIETY

1997

Published by
The Rissingtons Local History Society
Tallet House, Little Rissington, Cheltenham, Gloucestershire, GL54 2ND

Proceeds from sales of this book will go to The Rissingtons Local History Society

Copyright © Michael Boyes 1997

All rights reserved

ISBN 0 9530661 0 X

Designed and produced by Production Line, Minster Lovell, Oxford
Printed in Great Britain by Redwood Books, Trowbridge

CONTENTS

	Acknowledgements	5
1	**A New Beginning**	7
2	**The Early Years – Setting the Scene**	11
3	**Great Rissington National School**	16
4	**Developments in Education from 1860 to 1902**	19
	The Revised Code and 'Payment by Results'	19
	Attendance	21
	Education Legislation – 1870 to 1902	23
5	**Great Rissington Board School**	25
6	**Extracts from the School Board Minute Book – 1875 to 1896**	29
	Inspection Day	31
7	**The Building of the New School**	44
8	**The Final Years of the School Board**	51
9	**Great Rissington Council School – to 1920**	56
	The School Attendance Sub-Committee	61
	Discipline and Punishment	61
	Health and Fitness	63
	Reports by HM Inspector, 1906–1910	63
	The School House	66
	From 1912 to 1914	67
	The First World War	70
10	**The Years from 1920 to 1937**	77

11	**The Coming of the RAF and the Second World War**	88
	The Grice-Hutchinson War Diaries	90
	The Education Act, 1944	97
12	**The School from 1945 to 1958**	98
	A Separate RAF School	101
	The Threat of Closure	103
13	**Highlights from the Years after 1958**	107
	A New Headteacher	110
	A Time of Change	114

Appendices

1	The Standards of Examination laid down in the Codes of the Education Department	119
2	The Relative Value of Money and Inflation	121
3	School and Village Numbers	122

Notes   124

Bibliography   127

ACKNOWLEDGEMENTS

Permission to quote from source documents held by the following is gratefully acknowledged: Gloucestershire County Council for archives held at the Gloucestershire Record Office (GRO); the Church of England Record Centre, which holds the records of the National Society; the Public Record Office (PRO). Most of the documents referred to in this book which are held by the PRO are Crown copyright. My thanks also to: Mr. Sambell for giving me permission to reproduce photographs owned by Butt Studios of Bourton-on-the-Water; The Journal Series, Evesham: the Oxfordshire Photographic Archive; and The Photographer Ltd., Gloucester.

I am most grateful to all those who have lent me documents and who gave me permission to copy and use old photographs: Brian Agg, Dorothy Handy, Marjorie Hicks, Pamela Howse, Arthur Lane, Kay Lewis, Clare Mayo, Rita Minchin, Phil Pratley, Maude Pill, Mary Robbins, Michael Stratford, and Fred Webb.

Thanks are also due to the many people who have given me help and advice: David Bishop, Maggie Boyes, John Boyles of the Gloucestershire Health Authority, Peter Bullock, Doreen Clegg, Ruth Dawson, Rupert Duester, Sarah Duffield at the Church of England Record Centre, Elizabeth Franklin, Norman Good, Jane Hemmings, Phil Johnson, Elizabeth Lal at Stow library, Ralph Mann, Gordon Ottewell, David Viner at the Corinium Museum, all the staff at the GRO and those at the PRO at Kew, and all who agreed to be interviewed for this book.

Several people freely gave up their time to create designs and diagrams for this book; I thank Paul Clark both for designing the covers and for his valuable technical advice, and Norman Good and Mike Pennington for their individual drawings.

The publication of this book of local history would not have been possible without financial support from several organisations and individuals, and I am very grateful to the following for their contributions: Cheltenham and Gloucester Rural Initiative Fund, Cotswold District Council, Great Rissington Parish Council, The Langtree Trust, The Summerfield Charitable Trust, and Richard Turner. My thanks also to Jenny Surch and the committee of The Rissingtons Local History Society, Janne Bishop, Marion Couchman, Lesley Morgan, and everyone who has contributed in various ways towards the success of this publication.

Photographic work has been expertly processed by The Darkroom, Cheltenham; my thanks to Barry for his advice.

Cotswold District Council

The village green at Great Rissington, c.1905, with Mr Edwards, schoolmaster, and his family beneath the elm tree.

Great Rissington School, between 1910-1930, showing a separate entrance gate for girls and infants. A wall in front of the school separates the boys' playground from that for the girls and infants. *The Oxfordshire Photographic Archive, DLA, OCC.*

I

A NEW BEGINNING

'Anyone who can compare the demeanour of our young people at the present day with what it was five and twenty years ago must notice how roughness of manner has been smoothed away, how readily and intelligently they can answer a question, how the half hostile suspicion with which they regarded a stranger has disappeared; in fact how they have become civilised'.

An HM Inspector, 1895 - G.A.N. Lowndes, 'The Silent Social Revolution'[1]

A village school is very much a reflection of the community in which it finds itself. The story of a *Cotswold Village School from Victorian Times* gives some insights into how life has changed in a farming community over the last 150 years or so. This is an account of the development of education over that period in one rural village – Great Rissington – but much of this account could apply equally to other small villages in the Cotswolds and elsewhere.

Not long after the village school was rebuilt on a new site above the green in 1897, the Rev. Madan Pratt, chairman of the School Board, described a Christmas treat for the children. Writing in the *Stow Deanery Magazine* in February 1902, he captures something of the enjoyment of the occasion:[2]

'On Boxing day December 26th, Mr and Mrs Cooper (who are at present at Barrington Park) most kindly invited all the children attending the Sunday and Day Schools at Great Barrington, Taynton and Great Rissington to a Tea and Christmas Tree. Our children were all conveyed in wagons kindly lent by Mr Churchwarden Mace and Mr Sidesman Brook and arrived at Barrington Park at 3.30. Tea was partaken of, and afterwards all were taken to the tennis court, which was most beautifully decorated. The entertainment commenced with an exhibition of some wonderfully trained jugglers, who went through various balancing tricks, including bicycle riding, and ending with conjuring tricks; after this a Punch and Judy show, which all much enjoyed; then 'The Trees', three in number, laden with beautiful presents, which were distributed to the children by Mr and Mrs Cooper.'

The rector and his four daughters were accomplished musicians, and it was as a result of their interest and enthusiasm that regular concerts were held in the village during the early years of this century. Describing one such occasion in 1901, Mr Pratt wrote:

'What proved to be a most successful concert took place in the schoolroom on Wednesday evening, December 11th. The room was crowded with a large and appreciative audience, every available seat being taken, and many having to stand. The programme was a very long and attractive one, and included two songs and two duets by Miss Margaret Hicks-Beach, who was ably accompanied by her sister ... Mr Watts Lea, always a great favourite, was most amusing with his dry humour and gave four sketches, accompanying himself on the piano. The violin trio was well rendered, and the duologue – 'The Backward Child' – caused endless amusement. [A] musical Robinson Crusoe was most carefully given by members of the choir. Mr T.H. Mace, who was very appropriately dressed in skins, entering with the well-known dog Dan ... described in graphic language the life and adventures of Robinson Crusoe ... Thirty school children, with blackened faces and nigger dresses, under the able conductorship of Mr Holmes [schoolmaster], sang two plantation songs in a very pleasing manner. The entertainment concluded with Haydn's Toy symphony with full orchestral accompaniment.'

About a month later, the school was the venue for a dance, to which guests from other villages were invited:

'On Friday January 17th [1902] about 80 visitors assembled, some from Bourton-on-the-Water, Slaughter and Barrington and dancing was kept up from 9 o' clock until 4 am. The music was supplied by Mr Kirby, on a piano loaned by Mr Braye of the Wellington Hotel, Bourton. Mr Holmes kindly acted as caterer, and Mr Winfield as M.C., who at the close proposed a vote of thanks to the School Board and Mr and Mrs Holmes. The singing of 'God Save the King' closed an enjoyable evening.'

Later that year, the Rev. Madan Pratt described an outing for the village choir, many of whom were boys at the school. Both he and the new schoolmaster, Mr Edwards, were keen cricketers and Mr Pratt would often give the results of village cricket matches in the deanery magazine. In September 1902, he wrote:

'On August 19th, the rector took the choir (19 in number) to Cheltenham for the day to see [the] Gloucestershire v. Australians match. Mr Edwards (schoolmaster) and Mr William Smith (organist) accompanied the party. Through the kindness of Mr Churchwarden Mace and Mr Sidesman Brook, wagons were provided for the out and return journey to Bourton station to catch the 9.13 train. On arriving at Cheltenham, the party went by Electric Car to the foot of Cleeve Hill and back to Pittville Gardens, thence to dinner at the Waverley restaurant in High Street after listening to the Town Band in the Promenade. After an excellent dinner the party walked by Montpellier Gardens to the College cricket ground and witnessed the cricket match until 6 o'clock. Tea was then partaken of, and all returned home, much pleased with the day's outing.' From a later entry, we learn that the train home from Cheltenham to Bourton took two hours.

The choir and churchwardens with the Rev. Madan Pratt in 1908.
Also seated is William Smith, organist, who built the new school in 1897.
The choirboys attended the school and many of the men were past pupils.

Girls from the school dressed up for a concert, c.1919, in which Ruby Bartlett sang
'Goodnight Little Blue Eyes'. From the left: Mary Smith, Grace Hyatt, —,
Ruby Bartlett, Gladys Pratley, May Smith, Dolly White

With such inducements, it is not surprising that there was competition to get into the choir in those days. In addition to exciting outings, the boys were paid a farthing for each service they attended.[3] In 1904, the Rev. Madan Pratt wrote: 'The Choir all received a Christmas box, in addition to which Mr Edwards (schoolmaster) most kindly gave 2/- each to the two best behaved boys in the choir attending the Council School. These sums were given to Walter Souls and Ernest Duester'.

The school was at the heart of village life in the early years of this century. Not only was the building itself used for village concerts and other entertainments, but it was also the venue for various social functions. In December 1904, for example, the rector and Mrs Pratt gave their annual supper at the schoolroom, 'and 35 sat down to an excellent repast, being waited on by the ladies'. And events for the children were often occasions for the whole village to join in, as described by the rector in 1902:

'On Tuesday July 22nd, the school feast was held in the rectory grounds. The children assembled at the schoolroom at 3.30 and marched down to the Reading Room where the children's tea was prepared as the grass was somewhat wet. After which the teachers and many other friends had their tea at the rectory. Then followed games and sports of all kinds in a large meadow below the rectory. The rector and Mr Edwards being indefatigable in endeavouring to amuse all in various ways. The afternoon and evening fortunately turned out fine and a large number of the parishioners assembled and joined in the games, the tug-of-war causing much amusement. The day ended by the distribution of prizes (all in books) to children for regular attendance at Sunday School and cheers for the donors of the feast, each child was presented with a bun on leaving.'

Feasts and outings were not the only matters to feature in the *Stow Deanery Magazine*. Most of the parishioners of Great Rissington were relatively poor, and the following extract from January 1902 shows the extent to which many living in the village still benefited from regular charitable donations: 'The trustees of the United Charities of Great Rissington held a meeting in the schoolroom ... It was agreed to divide 10 tons 3 cwt. of coal equally between 58 houses; coats were given to Alfred Davis and Frank Mills; gowns to Mrs F. Pratley and Mrs John Howse; four yards of calico each to 58 persons. Webb's charity has been given to 50 children attending the Board School.'

The village now had a new school building, and the turn of the century brought with it a sense of hope for the future. For many, this was 'a new beginning'. But the story of Great Rissington School starts much earlier.

II

THE EARLY YEARS – SETTING THE SCENE

Great Rissington is an attractive Cotswold village on the side of a hill facing west and south across the Windrush valley, some three miles from Bourton-on-the-Water. The sloping landscape has given the parish its name, which signifies a hill overgrown with brushwood. This has long been a farming village, and it seems likely that wool merchants in Northleach bought wool from farmers in Great Rissington as early as the late fifteenth century.

In the seventeenth and early eighteenth centuries, Great Rissington would have been described as an 'open' parish, having a significant number of freeholders.[4] However, the number of freeholders declined in most agricultural parishes during the eighteenth century as major landowners bought up small farms which had ceased to be viable. The Enclosure Act for Great Rissington was passed in 1813, and the resulting award gave 1,389 acres to Lord Dynevor of Barrington Park, whilst the rector received 509 acres. The greater part of the award to the rector, 411 acres, was in compensation for giving up his

Great Rissington at the end of the nineteenth century, with the school on the far left, above the village green.

right to collect tithes. In addition, three farmers were awarded between 50 and 100 acres, six received awards of between 5 and 25 acres, and the remaining twelve owners received 1 acre or less each.[5]

The 1851 census is of interest as it was the first one to be completed after Great Rissington National School was founded. It shows that there were five farms of more than 250 acres and several smaller farms in the village. By now, the population had risen to 493, and more than 70% of males over the age of 14 were directly engaged in agriculture, mostly as labourers. At the age of 14 or earlier, children would work on the farms as ploughboys and shepherd boys, or as grooms. Other occupations in the village at this time included a mole catcher, tailors, shoemakers, servants, wheelwrights and blacksmiths, carpenters and masons, a shopkeeper, a beer seller, a butcher, a baker, a clock and watch maker, a dealer in earthenware, a dressmaker, a miller, a maltster, a fellmonger, and a school master and mistress. Three people were recorded as being in receipt of parish relief.

The village in those days was entirely self-supporting in dairy produce, meat, bread and vegetables. Wheat was grown for the villagers and beans and oats were grown in large quantities for the horses. Until the end of the nineteenth century, no milk was sent away from the village, as the number of dairy cows was just sufficient to meet demand. Any surplus milk was fed to the calves, and butter was sold at all the farms. A half-penny would buy a large jug of buttermilk on churning days.[6]

For entertainment, villagers could call in to one of the three inns that existed at that time. Everyday items were supplied by the general store, the baker and the butcher. The village also had a carpenter's shop, a blacksmith's forge and a cobbler's shop. The nearest doctor lived in Bourton, but few could afford his services in those days. The village was very much a self-contained community, where many families had lived for generations.

The Swan Inn, Great Rissington, in the early years of the twentieth century.

Wealth and power were enjoyed by the squire, Lord Dynevor, and his brother the rector, the Very Reverend, the Honourable Edward Rice. These two men played an important part in providing the funds necessary to establish a National School in Great Rissington, and their successors continued the philanthropic work. However, before the National School was built, others were at work in the village providing both day and Sunday Schools for the children of the poor.

The earliest record of any schooling in the village dates from 1739 when the rector, John Webb, gave £50 from which the interest was to be used for teaching six poor children to read.[7] The parochial returns to the Select Committee on the Education of the Poor in 1818 show that there was 'a school in which 30 children are instructed, six of whom are paid for by a bequest of Mr Welbs [sic] of £2 a year, and the rest by a subscription from the rector [Edward Rice] of £6 6s per annum'. There was also 'a day school of the better sort, consisting of 14 children', and 'a Sunday School containing 26 boys, and another 25 girls'. The entry for Great Rissington includes the following observation: 'The poor have sufficient means of educating their children'.[8] The census of 1811 gives the population of Great Rissington as 361, whilst the parochial return records the number of poor in 1815 as 53.

By the time of the Education Enquiry of 1833, the village had:

'*Three Daily Schools*; one of which contains 10 males and 16 females; another (commenced 1833), 11 males and 21 females; the former has an endowment of £2 per annum, being the interest of money left by Mr Welb *[sic]*, for the education of 6 poor children; to this the rector (the Dean of Gloucester) adds a sufficient sum for the education of 25 children; the remainder, in both schools, pay one penny per week, and the curate makes up the difference; the other is a small school, kept by a cottager, in which 12 children are instructed at the expense of their parents. – *Two Sunday Schools*, one with 30 males, the other with 23 females; both are supported by subscription.'[9]

Sunday Schools were the most widespread means of addressing the problem of elementary education in the years before 1833, when the State first took limited responsibility for education. The development of the Sunday School movement owes much to two men from Gloucestershire – Robert Raikes, an Anglican, and William Fox, a Baptist. Raikes was greatly influenced by his experience as a prison visitor and reformer. His visits to Gloucester Gaol confirmed his belief that there was a clear link between ignorance and crime. He determined to do something for 'the multitudes of wretches' (children), who, after working six gruelling days a week, 'spend their time in noise and riot ... cursing and swearing'.[10] With the help of his colleague the Rev. Thomas Stock, he opened his first Sunday School in Gloucester in 1780, and several others were to follow over the next couple of years. Although not the first to start a Sunday School, Raikes' achievement was to publicise and promote the benefits to be derived from such schools through the pages of his *Gloucester Journal*, thereby ensuring that a local initiative became a national movement.

For the Sunday School movement to grow, it needed a national organisation and it was here that William Fox played an important role. Born in Clapton-on-the-Hill of humble origins, Fox went on to make his fortune in commerce in London. In 1784, he bought the Clapton estate and immediately established a day school there for poor children. He read of Raikes' work in Gloucester and the following year he put forward plans for a Sunday School Society, with the inaugural meeting taking place in London. By 1833, the number of Church of England Sunday Schools in Gloucestershire had risen to 300 and those for Nonconformists had increased to 120.[11]

Sunday Schools in the early nineteenth century were intended to educate those who could not afford to provide education for themselves. In addition to religious and moral instruction, reading and writing were taught, and the Sunday School movement became almost entirely a working class institution. By 1851, it is estimated that some 2,100,000 children were enrolled in Sunday Schools in England, representing around 75% of working class children between the ages of five and fifteen.[12]

One of the most widely circulated books of poems that would have been used in Sunday Schools at that time was Dr Isaac Watts' *Divine and Moral Songs*. Many of these poems were used as a means of both religious instruction and social control. In 'Obedience to Parents', for example, children were warned of the consequences of not doing as they were told:

> Let children that would fear the Lord
> Hear what their teachers say:
> With reverence meet their parent's word,
> And with delight obey.
>
> Have you not heard what dreadful plagues
> Are threaten'd by the Lord,
> To him who breaks his father's law
> Or mocks his mother's word?
>
> What heavy guilt upon him lies!
> How cursed is his name!
> The ravens shall pick out his eyes,
> And eagles eat the same.

All was not doom and gloom, however; those children who worshipped God and honoured their parents would enjoy long lives on this earth, and 'hereafter too'.

Historically, the provision of education had been under the control or influence of the Church. Both the Charity Schools and Sunday Schools had close links with the Church, and in 1811 the National Society for Promoting the Education of the Poor in the Principles of the Established Church was established. Another voluntary society established around this time for the education of the poor was the British and Foreign Schools Society, which although non-denominational, was supported mainly by the Nonconformists. It was to these two voluntary societies that the first central government funds were made available for elementary education in 1833. A grant of £20,000 was made to aid private subscription for the erection of schools for the education of the children of the 'poorer classes'. By 1839, the grant had increased to £30,000 and a special Committee of the Privy Council was set up to administer the grant, with inspectors appointed to examine the work of the schools.

During the early part of the nineteenth century, there was much debate nationally about the wisdom of extending education to the poorer classes. The need to educate a rapidly rising population[13] to meet the requirements of an industrial and commercial age was opposed by many who feared that the ability to read seditious publications would lead the labouring poor to dissatisfaction with their place in society, or worse, to revolution. By the 1830s, statistics was a developing social science and a French statistician A.M. Guerry produced data which purported to show that there was a direct relationship between areas of high crime and high education.[14] Many conservatives interpreted the soaring crime rate as a function of education instead of the reverse, whilst liberals advocated education as a social cure-all. There were many who were still of the opinion that the prime purpose of elementary education was religious and moral, that children should be taught their duty towards God and 'their betters', to whom they should defer. Nevertheless, there was a growing recognition that if Britain were to prosper and compete in the new age of machines, improving communications and a broadening franchise, it was essential to extend the provision of education to all. But it was to be many years before the State enacted legislation requiring attendance by all children at elementary schools.

The main obstacle to the further development of a state education system at this time was sectarian animosity between the Church of England on the one hand, and Dissenters and Catholics on the other. The Anglicans believed that the Established Church should take the lead, and it provided more voluntary schools than any other agency. But the Nonconformists would not tolerate what they feared would be an Anglican monopoly.

The Factory Act of 1833 stipulated that children working in factories must attend school for two hours a day. In 1843, Sir James Graham proposed to reduce the hours of work of children to enable them to attend compulsory grant-aided schools either in the morning or the afternoon. These district schools would be placed under the control of the Established Church, although the ministers of the different denominations would have the right to give religious instruction to children whose parents asked for it. When the proposed Bill was made public, there was an outcry from both Protestant Nonconformists and Catholics. Despite attempts to amend the Bill to take account of the various concerns expressed, an agreed consensus could not be reached and so the education proposals were dropped.

There were still many, including the Prime Minister, Sir Robert Peel, who were opposed to the principle of State intervention in the provision of education. There was now a return to 'voluntarism'; subscription lists were opened for the building of schools, and money flowed in. However, government grants also increased significantly and by 1856 the annual grant paid to voluntary schools which accepted inspection had risen to £541,000.

III

GREAT RISSINGTON NATIONAL SCHOOL

Many schools were built during the mid-nineteenth century. In 1840, a small village school affiliated to the National Society was built in Little Rissington, and in the following year an application was made for a grant to build a school in Great Rissington. Such grants from the National Society formed only a small part of the total costs of building a school. In his letter requesting a grant, the rector, Edward Rice, wrote 'my brother Lord Dynevor is the owner of nearly the whole parish of Great Rissington. Whatever the expense is, must be paid by me and five pounds subscribed by my curate, as the occupiers of the houses are only farmers'.[15]

The land on which the school was to be built was a gift from Lord Dynevor to the rector, Edward Rice, and 'George Godfree and William Hyatt the churchwardens and the said William Hyatt and John Porter the overseers of the parish'.[16] The posts of churchwarden and overseer of the poor were of considerable importance in those days and were elected annually from the more substantial householders of the parish. Their responsibilities were defined by the Poor Laws which authorised them to levy a poor rate in the parish to meet the needs of the aged, needy and infirm. This role continued until the Poor Law Amendment Act of 1834 which brought to an end the system of granting poor relief except through the provision of a workhouse.

The conveyance agreement signed by Lord Dynevor stipulated that the land (measuring 'sixty feet on every side') be used 'as a site for a school for poor persons in the parish'. The school was 'to be under the management and control of the rector', and be open to inspection by Her Majesty's Inspectors.[17] The churchwardens and overseers were to be trustees.

Great Rissington village School was first established as a National School in 1842, on a site close to the church. It did not move to its present site above the village green until much later, in 1897. It is worth looking at the founding of the school in some detail. The application form submitted to the National Society shows that the new school was intended to receive at least 80 boys, girls and infants, although 'we hope [for] 100 of all ages during the week'.[18] There was to be one room with folding doors, which would be united during the week but which could be divided for use by the infants on Sundays. 'The boys' schoolroom is to be internally 17ft. 6in. long, 14ft. wide, and 12 or 14ft. high to the ceiling, making an area of 245 sq. ft. or 6 sq. ft. to each boy.' The room for the girls and infants was to be of the same dimensions. The building was to be of stone, with a stone slate roof, 'the regular roof of the county'. The estimated cost of the whole undertaking was £246 12s. 7d., of which £102 6s. 2d. was for labour, with the balance being the value of the ground and materials.

Instruction in the school was to be afforded by 'a penny a week [from each child] – and more is to be paid for writing and arithmetic'. The Terms of Union with the National Society stipulated that:[19]

1. 'The children are to be instructed in the Holy Scriptures and in the Liturgy and Catechism of the Established Church.
2. With respect to such instruction the schools are to be subject to the superintendence of the Parochial Clergyman.
3. The children are to be regularly assembled for the purpose of attending Divine Service in the Parish Church ... unless such reason be assigned for their non-attendance as is satisfactory to the managers of the school.
4. The masters and the mistresses are to be members of the Church of England.
5. A report on the state and progress of the schools is to be made, at Christmas every year, to the Diocesan Board, the District Society, or the National Society; and the schools are, with the consent of the managers, to be periodically inspected by persons appointed either by the Bishop of the Diocese, the National Society, or the Diocesan Board of Education.
6. In case any difference should arise between the Parochial Clergy and the managers of the schools ... respecting the religious instruction of the scholars, or any regulation connected therewith, an appeal is to be made to the Bishop of the Diocese, whose decision is final.'

The Church of St John the Baptist, Great Rissington, c.1900. *(GRO, GPS 268/2)*

Once these terms had been signed and agreed on 2nd June 1841, the National Society confirmed that it would make a grant of £20, and there was a further grant of £41 from the Committee of Council on Education, thus ensuring that the new school was completed free of 'any debt, charge or claim of any kind'.

The report of the Church School Inquiry of 1846-7 showed that there were 30 boys and 44 girls attending the National School at this time, though almost half of these attended only on Sundays.[20] The total paid to the master or mistress, 'including children's pence and any allowance for coal etc', was £30. According to the Inquiry report, there were also 18 boys and 16 girls attending dame schools in the village. Dame schools were often, though not always, run by women in their own cottages; the education given was usually of the most basic kind and the women were almost always unqualified.

It is clear from the preface to the published findings of the Church School Inquiry that the hierarchy of the Established Church was concerned that much remained to be done throughout the country to extend and improve the provision of education for the poor. It is probable that their concern was primarily for the moral well-being of the children, as indicated by the following comment: '[these returns] ... may stimulate all ... to more earnest exertions, and may encourage them to vigorous efforts in helping to feed the Lambs of Christ's flock with sound and religious nourishment.'

Whether the poor in Great Rissington were in any greater need of such moral and religious instruction than those elsewhere is not known. We do know that there were several convictions for offences committed by villagers around this time, including one serious enough to warrant transportation to Australia for seven years.[21] In February 1863 Joseph Baylis, an agricultural labourer aged 28, was convicted of stealing two fowls from Hulbert Lewin, a farmer in the village. For this offence, he was sentenced to two months hard labour.[22] A younger brother and sister of Joseph Baylis were listed as 'scholars' in the 1851 census, and it is possible that Mr Baylis (or Bailiss) – who we know could read – has the distinction of being the first former pupil of Great Rissington School to receive a prison sentence! His victim, Hulbert Lewin, was one of the first members of the School Board when it was formed in 1875. The word 'scholar' was used to denote any child attending school, not just the brightest ones.

IV

DEVELOPMENTS IN EDUCATION FROM 1860 TO 1902

From the time when Great Rissington National School was first established until 1876 when it became a Board School, very little information survives. However, the implementation of the Revised Code of 1862[23] brought about great changes in the work of Her Majesty's Inspectors (HMIs) and had a profound effect on the curriculum within all schools in receipt of a government grant. By understanding the provisions of the Code, we are able to gain a reasonably clear picture of what was taught at Great Rissington School for the next thirty years or so.

The Revised Code and Payment by Results

In 1857, a Royal Commission chaired by the Duke of Newcastle was appointed to look into the state of popular education and to advise on any measures that might be required for the extension of 'sound and cheap elementary instruction to all classes of the people'. The Commissioners estimated that the majority of children 'of the poorer classes' attending school left at the age of eleven, and that average school life was 4-6 years.[24] There was considerable demand for child labour and children were often absent or left school at an early age in order to contribute to the family income, as the Commission noted: 'When it is remembered that agricultural wages range from 9s. to 14s. a week and that children can add to this sum sometimes as much as 4s. or 5s. and generally 2s. 6d., the importance of their earnings to their parents becomes sufficiently apparent.'[25] Sometimes a child could earn even more; in October, for example, a child of twelve or thirteen could earn as much as 1s. a day for gathering potatoes.[26]

The government was anxious to obtain value for money, now that the annual grant had risen to over half a million pounds a year. The Commission concluded that many teachers were ineffective and others failed to concentrate enough on the basics. The Commission therefore recommended that every child in every school to which grants were paid should be examined each year by a competent authority to ascertain whether 'those essential elements of knowledge are thoroughly acquired, and to make the prospects and position of the teachers dependent to a considerable extent on the results of the examination'.[27]

It was partly to address some of the weaknesses identified by the Commission that

Robert Lowe, Vice-President of the Committee of Council on Education, introduced the Revised Code in 1862. Under the terms of the Code, grants were to be calculated on both attendance and the results of an annual examination conducted by HMIs, based on the three Rs. Such grants would henceforth consist of two parts: 4s. per child based on the number in average attendance; and a further 8s. per child over six years old for passes in the annual exam in reading, writing and arithmetic, with a deduction of 2s. 8d. for failure in each subject. Infants could produce a grant of 6s. 6d. without examination, in addition to their attendance grant. The Standards of annual attainment were laid down (see Appendix 1), and each child was expected to move up a Standard every year. No pupil could be examined twice in the same Standard. To qualify for grant, a school must be under a certificated teacher. Grants could be reduced or withheld altogether from a school with inadequate buildings or lighting, registers not kept properly, girls not being taught needlework, poor discipline, religious education not being taught properly, or if there were not enough pupil teachers.[28]

One of the aims of the Revised Code was to ensure that all children (and not just the brightest) received attention from the teacher, as all had to pass the annual exam if the maximum grant were to be earned. Another benefit of the Code was that general reading books had to be provided; often schools had relied largely on the Bible as the only reading material. However, the Revised Code was to have serious adverse effects on both the range of subjects taught, and the methods of instruction. Heavy emphasis was placed on rote learning of set passages and on cramming for examination. It was not unknown for knowledge to be literally beaten into children, though there is no evidence that this was the case at Great Rissington. But entries in the Little Rissington log book show that punishment was used regularly: 'Punished the boys of the Third Standard for carelessness in arithmetic. The boys of the said Standard are the dullest in the school. They are very slow at arithmetic and spelling'; and 'punished [two children] for careless dictation'.[29]

In an effort to overcome some of the limitations of the Code, additional grants for 'specific' subjects such as English grammar, history and geography were introduced in 1867; by 1875, these were converted into 'class' subjects, with the grant dependent on the proficiency of the whole class rather than that of each individual, and at the same time a further range of specific subjects was introduced, including mathematics, science, modern languages and domestic economy. In practice, however, the range of subjects taught in most village schools remained strictly limited for some twenty or more years after the introduction of the Revised Code, with the emphasis heavily on the three Rs, needlework for girls, and religious instruction. It remained quite a struggle for such schools to ensure both adequate attendance and successful progress through the Standards for the three Rs at the annual examination. Although some of the early log books for Great Rissington School are missing, we know from those for Little Rissington that both grammar and geography were taught as specific subjects in 1879, but following an adverse report from HM Inspector on progress in the basics, geography was dropped from the curriculum; it did not appear again until 1893. A similar return to the basics occurred at Great Rissington in 1878.

Attendance

Reading through the log books of Little Rissington and other village schools, it is clear that concerns about poor attendance preoccupied successive teachers in the latter part of the nineteenth and early twentieth centuries. Older children were often absent to help with haymaking, harvesting or gleaning, and the start and finish of the summer 'harvest' holidays were dependent on the commencement or completion of harvesting. For example, the harvest holidays varied in Little Rissington as follows:[30]

1882 – September 1st: 'School closing for the harvest holidays.'
October 13th: 'School reopened this week, a great many of the children not back on account of the harvest not yet over, also the weather being very wet.'
1887 – August 11th: 'School closed for harvest holidays.'
September 26th: 'Reopened the school after a holiday of six weeks.'
1893 – August 4th: 'School closes today for the harvest holidays [one month]. Attendance has not been so good this week owing to the harvest having already begun.'

It was not just around harvest time that school attendance was influenced by the farming cycle. Older children were often absent during late June or July, either fruit picking or helping in the hayfield, whilst younger children helped to scare away birds or 'pick stones'. Sometimes absences were condoned by the managers of the school, as the following entries for Little Rissington show: 'Attendance poor, owing to the three weeks holiday allowed to children over eight years of age during the haymaking season;' and later, 'many children stay away half-days which interferes with their progress – the School Attendance Committee allow the children to stay away one-fourth of their time.' And absences in March were not uncommon: March 19th 1880 – 'The attendance has fallen off very much this week, all the older children are kept at home, being employed in the fields.' Similar patterns of absence occurred at Great Rissington School.

In the years before attendance at elementary school became compulsory, a further deterrent to regular schooling for the children of poor farm workers was cost. The usual fee of 1d. or 2d. a week per child was sometimes hard to find out of a father's wage of about 9s. a week in the 1850s. The rector, Edward Rice, had tried without success to make his tenant farmers in Great Rissington pay more to their labourers, as the following extract from a letter to his solicitor in 1837 shows: 'I think the farmers are now well enough off for me to require my tenants to pay their old rents. I took off a shilling an acre from Hyatt and two from Roberts on condition that they hand their labourers nine shillings a week. They have never fulfilled their part ... '[31]

School pence continued to be a problem for many poor families until 1891, when elementary schooling became free. Although the fees were a burden, the loss of a child's contribution to the family earnings was of much greater concern. On small farms both sons and daughters were expected to help from an early age, and in most working-class families in Victorian times children helped with many household chores as soon as they were able. Whilst boys undertook the heavier tasks, older girls were sometimes kept home from school to look after younger children when 'their mothers are engaged in field work'.[32]

In addition to the demands of the farming cycle, the weather was often a cause of reduced attendance. At a time when the shoes and clothes of poorer children were often flimsy or inadequate and rough country roads could quickly become very muddy, children were often kept at home in wet weather. Again, the Little Rissington log books illustrate this: July 31st, 1880 – 'Attendance fallen off the end of the week owing to the stormy weather.' Such entries were commonplace after wet or severe weather, or after snow falls in winter. Most children walked home at lunchtime – the break between the morning and afternoon attendances was two hours – and back to school in the afternoon, thus increasing their exposure to inclement weather. In winter, a number of the infants would be kept at home during the severest months. Sometimes individual children were deemed to be 'too delicate to attend school in wet or cold weather'.

As if all this were not enough for the hard-pressed teacher to contend with, illness was another major cause of absence. In rural counties of England during the 1890s, children under five years of age accounted for about a quarter of all deaths.[33] Lower standards of personal hygiene, poor sanitation, overcrowded homes, inadequate heating and lack of medical care made children especially vulnerable to epidemic diseases such as whooping cough, measles and scarlet fever, which were both widespread and potentially dangerous. An outbreak of such common diseases in a village could lead to the school being closed for several weeks. Cases of diphtheria and tuberculosis also occurred from time to time, and ringworm was common. Children suffering from ringworm would be sent home, and sometimes children would also be sent home 'for being dirty' (as at Great Rissington in October 1871). The following log book entry for Little Rissington is typical of the problems facing teachers who were trying to prepare children for the annual examinations: 1894, January 11th – 'Attendance very poor, as there is much sickness among the children. The children seem very unfit for lessons, many present being far from well, and troubled with coughs and colds which cause great hindrance to their work in general.' When illness struck, children were often sick for long periods; Annie Smith returned to Great Rissington School in November 1877 after an absence of ten weeks. And if the master or mistress were ill, the school would also be closed.

At this time, school attendance figures were calculated on the number of attendances compared to the total number of occasions on which a school was open. Rather than have a poor attendance record when there were exciting events or distractions in the area, school managers would often grant a day or half-day holiday. Such holidays were given each year during Bourton Club week in June, or when the fair visited Bourton; other events for which half-day holidays were given included the local flower show, the Agricultural Show at Bourton, a meet of the hounds nearby, or a visit by the bishop.

The Revised Code laid down that a public elementary school must have met not less than 400 times a year, with each attendance being for not less than two hours of secular instruction. Only children with more than 200 attendances were eligible for grants on successful completion of the annual examinations in reading, writing and arithmetic. These requirements were later modified, but it was not until 1876 that attendance was made compulsory for every child at least to the age of ten, and every district without a School Board had to form an Attendance Committee for the purpose of compelling children to attend voluntary schools. The provisions of this Act were not consistently enforced, and consequently the Education Act of 1880 required all elementary school authorities to issue bye-laws enforcing attendance at school up to the age of ten, and thereafter to thirteen unless a child could be exempted on his record of attendances or by passing an examination, usually the 4th Standard.

The employment of children in agriculture was regulated by an Act of 1875,[34] which prohibited anyone from employing a child under eight (other than the child's parent on his own land). Children aged eight and nine were required to complete 250 school attendances in a year and those aged ten and eleven, 150 attendances. Morning school and afternoon school each counted as one attendance. In practice, however, the employment of young children was an important source of cheap labour for farmers and the provisions of this Act were very widely ignored.

The minutes of the Great Rissington School Board for May 13th 1882 mention a letter received from the Education Department in London 'in reference to the illegal employment of children, and also the irregular attendance of the same'.[35] At the following meeting in June, 'after much discussion ... it was unanimously resolved to carry out the law – by serving a notice to those persons neglecting to fulfil the same. The clerk was directed to follow up Charles Cyphus and Harry Cummins', the children concerned. There are frequent references to bad attendance in the subsequent minutes: March 1883 – 'The Attendance Officer was ordered to summon John Robinson for not sending his child to school regularly.' June 1883 – A report was made of bad attendances by children during the past two months. It was agreed 'that each child should make 30 attendances per month unless a reasonable excuse be given'. July 1885 – 'The clerk informed the Board that Alfred Hemming was fined 5s. on July 2nd for irregular attendance of his boy at school.'

Education Legislation – 1870 to 1902

When Mr Forster introduced the Elementary Education Act of 1870, he reported to parliament that "... only two-fifths of the children of the working classes between the ages of six and ten years are on the registers of the Government [aided] schools, and only one-third of those between the ages of ten and twelve".[36] Reliance on men of goodwill to undertake the building and maintenance of voluntary schools had failed to provide a place at elementary school for many children. The Act of 1870 sought to 'fill the gaps' in school provision, and thus a national system of elementary education became at last a matter for the State and not a form of charity.

The Act provided that wherever there were no elementary schools or the means to support existing schools, a School Board was to be elected triennially by the local ratepayers, with the power to levy an educational rate and to build a school as necessary. Such Boards would also receive government grants, and every child attending would pay a fee as laid down by the Board, but not exceeding ninepence a week. Attendance was not to be compulsory, but the Act allowed School Boards to make bye-laws requiring attendance between the ages of five and thirteen, with exemptions from the age of ten. They could also appoint Attendance Officers to follow up on truants.

On the contentious issue of religion, the Act provided a right of withdrawal from religious instruction on grounds of conscience in all public elementary schools, including those run by the churches. Furthermore, in all schools established by means of local rates, religious instruction was to be free of any particular denominational teaching. Such a restriction did not apply to Sunday Schools.

Whilst the Act of 1870 was an important measure to extend the provision of an elementary school place to all children, it did not widen the scope of what was taught. H.G. Wells commented that it was 'an Act to educate the lower classes for employment on lower class lines, and with specially trained, inferior teachers who had no university quality'.[37] Nevertheless, once the principle of universal elementary education had been established, further state intervention and control was inevitable.

Over the next thirty years, various Acts and Regulations were introduced which made elementary education compulsory (1876 and 1880), raised the *minimum* leaving age to eleven (1893) and then twelve (1899), replaced the system of 'payment by results' by grants dependent on average attendance (1890), and abolished elementary school fees which were replaced by an extra government grant (1891).

Despite all the progress that had been made, there was no unified structure for education in England and Wales, and there was inadequate provision and coordination of secondary education. It was to address these and other shortcomings that the Education Act of 1902 was implemented. Introducing the Bill in parliament, Mr Balfour said that 'this country was behind all its Continental and American rivals in the matter of education'. The Act made County and County Borough Councils the Local Education Authorities (LEAs), which were empowered to provide all secondary and technical education, and to coordinate all forms of education. School Boards were thus abolished. The most controversial measure – again on religious grounds – was the extension of rate aid to the hard-pressed voluntary (or Church) schools. On 1st April 1903, the management of Great Rissington and all other public elementary schools in Gloucestershire became the responsibility of the newly formed County Education Committee, consisting of 40 councillors and 20 others representing various educational interests.

V

GREAT RISSINGTON BOARD SCHOOL

One of the effects of the Education Act of 1870 was to stimulate the managers of National Schools to make great efforts to retain their independence. In 1871 Miss Mary Fellows, a certificated mistress who had trained in Cheltenham, was appointed to Great Rissington National School.[38] By now, the average attendance was 56, all of whom were taught in one room. The school was reorganised, but it appears to have been unsatisfactory and there was competition from a dame school in the village run by Mrs Esther Hemming, wife of the tailor.[39] It is interesting to note that in *Kelly's Directory*, Mrs Hemming was recorded as the mistress of the National School in 1856; she was still mistress in 1859, but by 1867, Mrs Maria Collett had been appointed mistress of the National School. The National School had an endowment of £5 a year, but 'was chiefly supported by the rector, the Rev. Henry Rice MA'.[40] In the village, there were also 'several small charities, given in clothes, linen etc, to the poor annually'.

It seems likely that as Mrs Hemming was not a certificated teacher, she could not have continued as mistress of the National School. It was a condition of the Revised Code that, to be eligible for a government grant, a school must be run by a certificated teacher. It is probable that Mrs Hemming was able to attract some children to her dame school who might otherwise have attended the National School. By 1874, a Miss Swift was the teacher at the National School, which came in for considerable criticism that year from HM Inspector:[41]

– 'I am very sorry to be unable to say anything in favour of this school except that Miss Swift seems to be a thoroughly conscientious teacher, who is honestly doing her best under the greatest disadvantages. The results of Standard work barely reach 50%; the Infants are indifferently taught, and suffer from the want of a classroom. Singing is just passable, needlework fair as far as it goes, but needing a better supply of materials for practice. I must add that the pupil teacher's geography paper betrays the most astounding ignorance and carelessness; the rest of her papers are fair. One tenth is deducted [from the annual Grant] ... for general inefficiency.'

It is interesting to note that the amount of grant received included the sum of £4 18s. 3d. for an 'evening school', which seems to have been discontinued soon afterwards.

It is possible that there were concerns about the National School in Great Rissington at this time, for some boys walked about three miles each way to attend school in Great Barrington, as the following entry in the Barrington log book indicates: Jan. 4th 1875 – 'The boys from Rissington [are] so frequently late at morning school; threatened to send them back home if after this week there is not an improvement; some late 3 and one 4 times this week'. The following week three of the Rissington boys were a quarter of an hour late and were duly sent home, resulting in a letter of complaint from one of the parents. It is not surprising that a period of wet weather subsequently caused 'irregularity in attendance of distant boys'.

In July 1875, the mistress commented in the log book 'that the third classroom [were] very backward in their reading. Found occasion to punish Elijah H. for being obstinate'.[42]

Following the 1870 Act, an Inspector's report had determined that school accommodation was required for 82 children in Great Rissington. This assessment was based on a village population of 481, 'of whom $6/7$ths are of the class whose children may be expected to attend elementary schools'.[43] In the village, only the National School was recognised to be an efficient school, and accommodation within it was deemed to be sufficient for 62 children. There was therefore a need to build an additional classroom in order to make available adequate school accommodation at an efficient school within the parish.

Attempts to raise money locally to build the extra classroom were unsuccessful. There were just 21 ratepayers in the village in 1873. On 7th January 1875, the Education Department in London issued a Final Notice to say that if the additional school accommodation were not provided within six months, a School Board would be compulsorily formed.[44] In September, the Rev. Henry Rice wrote to say that nothing had been done, as 'I cannot get the farmers to contribute',[45] and a School Board was duly formed towards the end of 1875. The National School, in its building near the church, now became a Board School funded by a combination of government grants, local rates and school fees. The manager of the National School, Henry Rice, agreed to transfer the school to the Board for a term of 50 years 'at a nominal rent of 5/- per annum'.[46] Continuity was maintained by the appointment of Henry Rice as chairman of the new School Board. He reserved the right to use the school premises on Sundays and in the evenings.

It must, nevertheless, have been a disappointment for the Rev. Henry Rice when his control (and thus that of the church) was diluted by the election of a School Board for the parish. The influence of squire and parson over a rural village at this time was still very considerable. Long-established patterns of deference and obligation to the manor house and vicarage still prevailed. In Great Rissington from 1789 to 1897, there were only three rectors and they were all relations of the lords of the manor at Barrington Park. The living at Great Rissington was in the gift of Lord Dynevor, owner of Barrington Park and the villages of Great Barrington and Great Rissington. Edward Rice, rector at the time that the original school was established, was a brother of Lord Dynevor; without their support, the school would not have been built. Edward Rice resigned in 1856 in favour of his son Henry, who lived in the rectory with his wife and children until he died in 1896. With the death in 1869 of George Rice Rice-Trevor, Baron Dynevor, the Barrington estate passed to Edward Rhys Wingfield, the son of one of the late Baron's daughters. Thus at the time that the Great Rissington School Board was set up, the village was still very much under the influence and patronage of the squire, Edward Wingfield, and his relative, the Rev. Henry Rice.

Henry Rice was almost certainly a wealthy man. He was the incumbent of a very comfortable living which included more than 500 acres of land, employing a Mr Henry

Haymaking on Manor Farm in the early 1920s.
From the left: Albert Agg, Charlie White, —- Ernie Agg, —- Jack Robinson, —-
On the ladder: George Pill (top), Mr Agg

Spencer as his farm bailiff. He also owned the land on which the National School stood. At least six staff were employed within the rectory, including a governess, a domestic nurse, a cook and several maids. However, with his wealth and position came an obligation to help those in need.

Both the rector and his family played an active part in the life of the school; in addition to being chairman of the new Board, Henry Rice frequently visited the school and gave talks. Each year he gave prizes for good work, and hair ribbons were given to the older girls to encourage tidiness. His wife and two unmarried daughters, Miss Beatrice and Miss Georgina, also visited and examined needlework completed by the girls and inspected their fingers and nails to make sure that they were clean.[47] Sometimes the Misses Rice would come into school and listen to the children sing or recite poetry. In addition, Miss Beatrice visited sick children in their homes, or comforted the small children in school when they cried by giving them apples or sweets. She also brought cough mixture and 'tooth tincture' when needed.[48] Both daughters sometimes helped with the feeding of the children by making soup, initially in the rectory kitchen and, after 1885, in the newly built Reading Room. In view of such patronage, it is perhaps not surprising that due deference was offered by the schoolgirls, who were taught to curtsey when they met the rector or his family.

Whilst the daughters of the rector and those of one of the farmers were taught by a governess until they were old enough to go away to school, the children of the working class families attended the Board School in the village. The Admissions Register for 1876 survives,[49] and below is an analysis of the occupations of the parents of the 88 pupils (from

44 different families) on the register during that year; this analysis has been checked against the 1881 census returns for the village:

Occupation of parent	Frequency
Agricultural labourer	25
Farmer	4 (includes 1 guardian)
Shepherd	2
Innkeeper	2
Carter	1
Wheelwright	1
Servant (f)	1
Shoemaker	1
Mason	1
Butcher	1
Baker	1
Machinist	1

The occupations of the parents or guardians of three children in the above analysis are unknown; excluding these, 80 per cent of the families with children at the school in 1876 were employed in agriculture and associated trades.

Analysis of the occupations of parents of the 87 children admitted to the school in the years 1882-84 shows that 34 were listed as labourers, and there were 3 publicans, 3 farmers, 1 farm bailiff, 1 blacksmith, 1 slater and 1 housekeeper. This was the period following the Education Act of 1880 which made school attendance compulsory at least to the age of ten. The intake for 1882 was 34, ranging in age from four to eleven, which indicates that some of the older children were attending school for the first time.

In the fifteen years between 1877 and 1892, the following *additional* occupations (with frequencies), were also recorded: shepherd – 7, gamekeeper – 2, shopkeeper – 2, cowman – 1, porter – 1, tailor – 1, schoolmaster – 1. Almost all of these parents were listed as living in Great Rissington.

Besides the rector, the other members elected to the School Board in 1875 were John Godfree, Hulbert Lewin and John Kerman – all farmers, and Albert Smith – wheelwright and blacksmith. Mr John Osborn was appointed clerk to the board, at a salary of £10 a year.

VI

EXTRACTS FROM THE SCHOOL BOARD MINUTE BOOK 1875 TO 1896

The early minute books, though often sparingly written and lacking in detail, nevertheless give us a good insight into the management of the school at that time.[50] What they do not give us is a picture of what went on in the classroom. For that we need the log books, and in their absence, reference is made to other material, including HM Inspectors' reports and occasional insights from the Little Rissington log books for the period.

There is no record in the minute books of the school hours, which could vary from one village to the next. At Little Rissington, the afternoon period was from 2 – 4.15 p.m. in summer and, because of fading light in the classroom, 1.30 – 3.45 p.m. in winter. The afternoon hours at Great Barrington were fifteen minutes longer, from 2 – 4.30 p.m. in summer and 1 – 3.30 p.m. in winter. It seems likely that the morning sessions were from 9 a.m. to noon in summer and earlier in winter, with a two hour break between the morning and afternoon attendances. Registers were taken twice a day.

The first meeting of the Board took place on November 4th 1875, but apart from the election of officers, there was no other business. At their next meeting, it was proposed 'that application be made to the trustees of the National School to let to the School Board the use of the school and premises for the purpose of a Board School'. It was also 'proposed that an advertisement be inserted in one of the usual papers for a certificated mistress at a salary of fifty pounds and a proportion of the grant'.

1876

Jan. – The Board agreed to meet in future on the second Friday in each month at 5.30 p.m.

Feb. 15th – 'The services of mistress Iyan were engaged with effect from 17 April, and the Board resolved that she should receive a salary of sixty pounds per annum and furnished apartments.' The proposal to make part of her salary dependent on grant earned was not implemented.

May 12th – It was agreed 'that the school children should pay the sum of two pence each for the eldest and one penny each for the others'. These sums were to be paid quarterly.

– Annie Smith commenced her duties as pupil teacher; previously, she had been a monitor. (Pupil teachers served a five year apprenticeship in an elementary school and had to pass exams each year, before going on to a teacher training college. Pupil teachers normally received a salary of £10 in their first year, increasing to £20 at the end of their fifth, providing that they passed their annual examination.)

May 20th – It was resolved that 'Hannah Day be engaged to clean the school for six months, and to receive one pound six shillings for the half year'. This was increased to 3d. per day or 1s. 9d. per week in November.

June 16th – The rent of the school was agreed at 5/- per annum, this sum being payable to Henry Rice, rector and chairman of the School Board.

June 27th – It was agreed that the National Society in London be paid £5 6s. 9d. for books and apparatus. The following bills were also paid:

for advertisements	18s.	
for cleaning	10s.	(to Mr Godfree)
for mending windows	2s.	
for cleaning school	7s.	(to Hannah Day)
for new brooms	3s.	
	£2 0s. 0d.	

July 14th – Mary Blower, aged 11, was appointed as a monitor at the rate of 6d. a week. (This was later raised to 9d. The use of a few older children as untrained monitors enabled a single certificated teacher, aided by a pupil teacher, to control large classes or a whole school with an age range – including infants – from 4 to 13. The payment by results system of grants, out of which the teacher's salary had to be paid, often acted as a disincentive to the employment of additional adult teachers).

Aug. 11th – A holiday of one month (to September 9th) was granted.

Oct. 13th – The yearly accounts showed a balance in hand of £2 0s. 1d.

Oct. 27th – The Education Department in London approved and the Board accepted Mr Earle's tender of £144 13s. for the building of a new classroom for the infants. The Board had been unable to comply with Section 7 of the 1876 Education Act, 'on account of insufficient room'. The single classroom, when full, would have been occupied by some eighty or more children and infants, and in winter only those closest to the one fire were able to keep warm; from time to time, those furthest from the fire would change places with those nearest. – The clerk was authorised to order more coal and coke to heat the school.

Dec. 8th – It was resolved that copy books be obtained and 'sold to children whose parents can afford it, at cost price, 2d. each, left to the discretion of the schoolmistress'.

Dec. 16th – It was resolved to borrow the money for building the infant classroom from the Public Works Loan Board, to be repaid over ten years by ten equal instalments. The interest rate was $3\frac{1}{2}\%$.

1877

March 9th – The sum of £35 was received from the Rating Authority. At this time, rates were only paid by occupiers of land. It was noted that 'the teachers of this school have given satisfaction'.

April 6th (Log book) – 'Frederick Smith was sent home on Friday morning through a stone having been thrown at him by one of the workmen engaged about the classroom'.

Inspection Day

March 28th – The school was examined by HM Inspector, Percival Balmer.

The day of the annual inspection was anticipated with dread by pupils and teachers alike. The inspectors, with their university degrees, were divided from teachers by virtue of their background in a class-conscious society; it was felt that inspectors had to be the social equals of the managers of the school, and for this reason teachers, who were generally of a more humble background, were not appointed as inspectors at this time.[51]

The date of the inspection was known in advance, and the preceding weeks would have been spent practising the type of questions that the Inspector would ask. The requirements of the Revised Code meant that teachers perceived the Inspector as an enemy instead of a counsellor and adviser. One result of this was that teachers would often pass on to other local schools where the inspection had yet to take place the arithmetic questions used by the Inspector. The examination thus became what Matthew Arnold, an Inspector himself, described as 'a game of mechanical contrivance in which the teachers will and must learn how to beat us'.

On the big day, the children would all be wearing their best clothes and be on their best behaviour. Examples of needlework would be laid out for the Inspector to examine. Those children who had registered more than 200 attendances would be presented for examination, starting with the lowest Standard. The Inspector would try to ensure that there was no cheating, warning of the dire consequences of copying, and in the process would add to the atmosphere of tension. The youngest children would be lined up, often standing back-to-back to prevent copying, with their slates, pencils and a reading book ready for dictation, arithmetic and reading tests.[52] Meanwhile, the other Standards would try to continue with normal lessons so that the Inspector could also assess discipline within the school.

There was inconsistency in both the standards and methods used by Inspectors; some would dictate excessively long sums so as to test both notation and arithmetic, e.g. Standard 3 – Take 5291236 from 8265075, or Standard 4 – Divide £46,983 13s. 8¼d. by 67.[53] However, HMI Balmer, who also inspected Little Rissington School, appears to have been reasonably sympathetic in his approach to the annual examination. Perhaps he was mindful of the requirement in Article 4 of the Revised Code that 'the object of the grant is to promote the education of children belonging to the classes who support themselves by manual labour', or to the instruction that each school should be judged on its 'whole character and work', including 'its religious, moral and intellectual merits'.

The Code of 1875 exhorted teachers 'to bring up children in habits of punctuality; of good manners and language; of cleanliness and neatness; and also to impress upon them the importance of cheerful obedience to duty, of consideration and respect for others, of honour and truthfulness in word and act'. As part of his overall assessment of a school, the Inspector would also try to form an impression of its moral character. Many schools and parents of today might wish they could return to these requirements of the 1875 Code.

So that the children and teachers could recover from the stress of the annual inspection and examination, a day's holiday was sometimes granted, as was the case at Great Rissington in March 1873.

May 11th – The Inspector's report had been received, which the Board 'considered to be satisfactory'. The report stated:

– 'The interval between the closing of the National School and its re-opening by the Board has doubtless told on the children. Still, they have done well on the whole and the Infants show, also, proof of careful teaching. The room is far too crowded for easy working and the enlargement should be completed with as little delay as possible. A second set of books and primers for the Infants, also additional slates and new maps must be provided at once. The girls should be taught to fix their own needlework ... '

– 'Twelve secular songs, at least, should be known, in order to earn the Grant under Article 19(a) for another year.' The Inspector also commented that the Admissions Register had not been completed properly.

June 15th – It was agreed that the Rev. Henry Rice be paid the sum of £20 for the whole of the school fittings (including desks, stove, clock, blackboard, maps, books), 'Mr Rice being the late manager of this National School'.

July 13th – School pence received by the treasurer for the quarter amounted to £4 8s. 7d.

– It was agreed 'that two stench traps be laid in the closets'. (According to *Great Rissington 1857 – 1957*, the log books of this period contained frequent references to 'stenches' and 'bad smells'. The privies were almost certainly earth closets, below which was a pit that would have had to be cleared out from time to time.)

Sept. 14th – The harvest holiday was prolonged by one week to six weeks, because harvesting had not been completed.

Oct. 12th – Mrs Lake was engaged as a seamstress at sixpence per afternoon, for eight days only. She lived in the village and gave her occupation as dressmaker in the 1881 census.

Oct. 19th – Bye-laws were drafted and sent to the Education Department for approval, adopting Standard 4 as the level to be achieved if a child wished to leave to work full time, and Standard 3 for 'half-timers'.

Dec. 14th – The clerk was authorised to obtain books, primers, calico and knitting needles required in the school. Unbleached calico was sent from the rectory from time to time for the girls to make 'shifts and drawers'.[54]

1878

The annual income and expenditure for the school year ended 28th February 1878 was as follows:[55]

Income

	£ s. d.
Grant from Committee of Council on Education	33 0 10
Rates	86 0 8
School fees	16 19 11
Books sold to children	2 0
Total	136 3 5

Expenditure

	£ s. d.
1 Salaries	
a) Teachers	60 0 0
b) Pupil teachers	14 12 8
c) Monitors	2 0 7
2 Books, apparatus and stationery	13 7 9
3 Fuel and light	4 18 1
4 Replacement/repairs to furniture, and cleaning	27 0 6
5 Repairs to buildings	7 13 10
6 Rent, rates, taxes and insurance	Nil
7 Other expenses:	
Mrs Esther Hemming, apartment for schoolmistress	6 10 0
Total	136 3 5

It is interesting to note that income and expenditure balanced exactly. The element of income that could be varied was the rates, and the rating demand was much higher in 1878 than in subsequent years. There is no doubt that a high rate would have been unpopular in a small agricultural village with few rate payers. In the following year, income from rates had been reduced to £52 3s. 2d., with total expenditure reduced accordingly. Income from rates remained at around £50 to £55 per annum for the next twenty years or so, before falling still further.

Feb. 8th – The Board resolved that 'the education in this school be confined to reading, writing, arithmetic, singing and needlework'. (This was a very limited curriculum, even by the standards of the day; we may assume that the Board was concerned that insufficient progress was being made in these basic subjects, upon which depended a substantial part of the government grant.) There also appears to have been some concern about the 'conduct, character and attention to duty' of Miss Iyan, the schoolmistress. The matter was put to a vote, with two Board members voting that they were satisfied and one voting no.

March 8th – 'The clerk read a letter from Miss Iyan wishing to resign her office, accepted March 30th'. Also on that day, Emily Townsend was engaged as a monitor, at 9d. a week.

April 6th – Mr E.R. Wingfield agreed to let a piece of ground measuring 310 square yards to the school 'for the purpose of a playground for the children'. The rent was 1s. a year, and the lease was for 21 years. (Due to the Victorian sense of propriety, there was a requirement at this time that there be a separate playground for boys and girls.)

May 29 – A summary of the Inspector's report was received:

'I am glad to find that since last year, a class-room has been added on to the school buildings. This is a great improvement and was much needed. The needlework and discipline are very fair. No extra subjects are at present attempted, and I think, wisely. The Standard children did fairly well in the elementary subjects, with the exception of the Third Standard children who are very backward. The writing in the First Standard is also below the mark. The younger children require rather more attention, some of them being in a backward state, though some show careful teaching.'

The songs presented to the Inspector at the examination included, 'Merry Dick', 'The Lightning's Flash', 'The Canadian Boat Song', 'The Soldier's Motherless Daughter', 'Will you come with me', and for the Infants, 'Little Letty' and 'Chatterbox'.

June 14th – The school was closed for Whitweek. – Funds received by the treasurer included:

books sold to children	1s. 3d.
two trees sold to Mr A Smith	5s. 0d.
gate & post sold to Mr Henry Rice	3s. 0d.

July 6th – Annie Smith was promoted to assistant teacher at the rate of £30 per annum, subject to three months notice on either side.

August 9th – The clerk was directed to see John Robinson about his son breaking a window.

– Amongst the accounts to be paid was one for 'the use of two and a half chains of land for 18 months to dig and stack stones for building purposes – £1'.

Sept. 28th – Mrs Morris was appointed as mistress on a temporary basis at a salary of 25s. a week, plus travelling expenses to and from London; railway fare, two journeys, 16s. 8d. – by road, 7s. 6d. Meanwhile, the search for a certificated mistress continued.

Nov. 1st – Miss E. Thorneley (certificated 2nd class), was appointed mistress at a salary of £60 p.a. plus furnished apartments.

Nov. 9th – The schoolmistress was asked to 'use her discretion in giving away eight pinafores as presents to children attending most of the time'. Also, forty children were recorded as absent through sickness. Later, Dr Moore of Bourton was asked to provide sick certificates, to be filed with the exam papers. (John Moore was a skilful surgeon who retired from practice in 1888. He founded the Cottage Hospital in Bourton in 1861. On his death, the local paper wrote that 'he freely devoted his professional ability and skill to benefit the sick poor in this and the surrounding parishes').[56]

1879

March 14th – The Board agreed to give shirts and pinafores as prizes to those children who had passed their annual exam and also made the most attendances.

Sept 29th – A proposal to build a lobby was deferred 'on account of the present [agricultural] depression'.

– It was also agreed that 'Miss Thorneley and Miss Smith be asked to use their influence with the children with respect to their manners in the street, both going and coming to school'.

1880

April 9th – The clerk was instructed 'to insure the school and classroom for £250, books and fixtures of all kinds, £50, total £300'.

July 9th – Although the agricultural depression was not over, the Board agreed 'to erect a small lobby for the convenience of boys' hats. Chiefly of wood with pine cover, small window and door, bottom to be paved with tiles'.

1881

A list of 'object lessons' for the Infant Class[57] for this year included such diverse objects as a Chameleon, Zebra, Humming Bird, Shark, Oyster & Mussel, Sponge & Coral, Copper, The Senses, a Tea-pot, Silkworm, a Looking Glass, Butter, and Stork (the bird). Altogether, the list included 30 objects, each of which would have been the subject of a separate lesson throughout the year. Object lessons were a form of very elementary science, and as the years progressed, the range of objects was extended.

Jan. 20th – A severe snow storm, with drifts from 4 to 8 ft. deep, kept most children away from school.

Feb. 11th – A complaint by the mistress, Miss Thorneley, that 'she was not treated with the deference she was entitled to by Miss Smith' was upheld by the Board, after listening to statements by both parties. It appears that the assistant teacher was under the impression that she was only answerable to the orders of the Board.

March 25th – The Board decided to give Annie Smith, assistant teacher, three months' notice, 'the object of this notice is to relieve the expenses of the Board'. The Board (which included Annie Smith's father) recorded that they were 'perfectly satisfied with the general good conduct of Miss Smith', and would be happy to supply her with a testimonial.

June 10th – Annie Gillett (age 13) was appointed as a full time monitress at one shilling a week, and Jane Goodway (age 14) was appointed as a part-time monitress at sixpence a week. (Dilution of staff experience is not new, it seems. Annie Gillett was later promoted to pupil teacher at £5 p.a.)

1882

It is clear from the minutes that the Board experienced many staffing problems over the years. In response to an enquiry from the Education Department in London, the Board recorded that 'the principal teacher's conduct and attention to duty was considered satisfactory'. One is left to speculate how the Education Department came to make such an enquiry, some months before HM Inspector's annual visit.

March 18th – 'The [Inspector's] report on the school was read and considered very satisfactory.'

June 9th – The number of children present at the school this week was 76.

June 16th – The clerk reported that Alfred Hemming's children had not attended in the past week, nor had they yet paid the school fees due. Written notice was delivered to the parents to send their children to school and pay the fees, or they would be summoned.

July 4th – After threatening to resign, Miss Thorneley persuaded the Board to pay directly to her the accommodation allowance of 2s. 6d. a week or £6 10s. p.a. paid to Mrs E. Hemming, thus enabling her to find her own apartment. This was the same Mrs Hemming who ran her own dame school until approximately 1880, and who had previously been mistress of the National School for several years.

Aug. 19th – William Smith, aged 34 and a plasterer by trade, was appointed clerk at £10 p.a. and also Attendance Officer at a further £2 p.a. (He later built the new school above the village green, and retained the post of clerk – and subsequently correspondent – for more than 35 years. A man of many talents, he became organist at the parish church, and also ran his own photographic business in the village.)

1883

March 2nd – It was agreed that the schoolmistress could sell needlework that was usually given away to the children, and then buy prizes with the proceeds. The accounts show that the sale of needlework became a useful source of extra income for many years to come.

July 16th – John Lake, John Tucker, Richard Porter and Alfred Hemming were summoned to answer to the Board for the bad attendance of their children. It was also resolved that J. Cummins be ordered to send his son to school, as he had not passed Standard 3. (The minutes contain many such references to the problems of poor attendance. In many rural communities, the Education Acts were unpopular and there was resentment at attempts to enforce school attendance; it seems likely that this was the case at Great Rissington. Sometimes, after repeated warnings to the parents by the clerk, William Smith, summonses were served for persistent non-attendance. There is an account in *Great Rissington 1857-1957* of two angry mothers in the 1890s walking to the court at Stow-on-the-Wold, and after being fined a shilling, threatening to duck the clerk in the pond. Apparently, the threat was never carried out, but the incident is indicative of the strong feelings aroused in farming villages in the years following the introduction of compulsory attendance at elementary schools.)

Nov 9th – Following Miss Thorneley's resignation, the Board appointed Miss Jane Greenwood as mistress, from the four letters of application and testimonials considered. Her salary was £50 p.a. plus the lodging allowance of £6 10s. a year.

1884

Feb. 27th & 28th – The annual inspection took place over two days.

April 18th – The clerk wrote to the Education Department seeking their agreement to allow the Board themselves to conduct the next triennial election of Board members, without the services of a returning officer. The purpose of this request was to 'relieve the expenses of the Board'. Permission was refused, and the accounts later show that £4 3s. was paid to Mr Francis for election expenses, a considerable sum. To put this in perspective, the same accounts show that the sum of 4s. was raised from the sale of needlework.

July 11th – The Board agreed to remit the school fees of Helen Webley until further notice. (Although the Board was empowered to remit fees in cases of hardship, very few such cases are recorded in the minutes.)

1886

Jan 15th – The Rev. Henry Rice requested payment of rent, rates and taxes on the school premises from 1876 to the present. This request caused some disagreement among the members of the Board, and consideration of the matter was twice deferred to later meetings. At the meeting on May 6th, bills from Mr Rice and Mr Wingfield were again presented. A compromise that the claim for six years be paid was put to a vote; two members were for, two against, so the chairman (none other than Mr Rice) used his casting vote in favour of payment. A cheque was drawn for £3 16s. 4d. to Mr Rice and one for 6s. for E.R. Wingfield.

Aug. 27th – The Board's staffing problems continued, following the resignation of the mistress, Miss Greenwood. They agreed to advertise for a certificated master and wife. The following advertisement was placed in *The Schoolmaster*:

> October 11th — Certificated Master, Board School
> Average [attendance] 70. Wife under Article 84
> Salary £75, Lodgings. – Address, Clerk
> Great Rissington, Gloucestershire

The professional journal in those days was *The Schoolmaster*, rather than *The Teacher* as it is now called. Whilst a schoolmistress was acceptable if unmarried, or married to the schoolmaster, the status of a married female teacher was often unacceptable within a traditional village community. *Kelly's Directory* for the period shows that the majority of village schools in Oxfordshire, Dorset and Wiltshire had one qualified, unmarried teacher.[58] The appointment of qualified unmarried female teachers, who were paid less than men, was often preferred by school managers short of money. However, because of the high turnover of unmarried female teachers, the Great Rissington Board decided to look for a master, with his wife acting as an unqualified 'supplementary' teacher. The use of female 'supplementaries' was allowed under the Code, provided that they were over eighteen, had been vaccinated against smallpox, were approved by the Inspector, and were 'employed during the whole of the school hours in the general instruction of the scholars'.

Sept. 10th – The Board offered the job of headmaster to Mr Edward Tennant, with his wife acting under Article 84, after considering applications and testimonials from seven schoolmasters. He accepted the job after travelling to see the school. Mr Tennant remained as headmaster for almost four years, and was remembered with 'respect and affection by the old people in the parish who were his pupils'.[59]

1887

March 8th – The books of account were audited at Stow, the audit stamp costing £2. Additional sources of income received during the year included:

	£	s.	d.
Sale of needlework	1	0	11
Sale of exercise books		7	9

The total income for 1887 was £115 19s. 10d., with school fees contributing some 11%.

Nov. 4th – The Board agreed to keep the school open for the time being, despite a letter from the sanitary authorities requesting the closure of the school owing to an outbreak of scarlet fever in the village.

Dec. 17th – 'The school bell having been carelessly broken by some youths, the clerk was instructed to inform them they must bear the expense of recasting, or further steps will be taken in this matter'.

1888

Dec. 24th, Christmas Eve – 'Complaints having been made from time to time of indecent behaviour on the school premises, two boys were now brought before the Board charged with the same. They ... confessing their guilt, the Board resolved to view the matter leniently and after severely censuring them for their conduct, ordered each to pay eighteen pence for [the] school cleaner in default of which further steps will be taken.'

1889 April 20th – HM Inspector suggested that a new set of reading books was much needed, and the Board agreed to order new ones. The inspectors often made recommendations aimed at raising standards or improving the physical environment within the school itself, but their advice was not always heeded.

1890

July 19th – A letter was sent to Mr John Garne advising him that he was no longer recognised as a member of the Board 'having absented himself from all meetings of the Board for 21 successive months'. John Garne came from a long-established family of Cotswold yeomen farmers. He began farming at the age of 54, and became tenant of a large farm at Great Rissington. He was re-elected to the Board in October 1893, and became chairman briefly following the death of Henry Rice in 1896, before his own death the next year.

Sept. 6th – After advertising in *The Schoolmaster* for a replacement for Mr Tennant following his resignation, the Board considered applications from twelve candidates. Mr A. Davies was appointed headmaster, with his wife to act as a supplementary teacher, at a joint salary of £75 plus an unchanged lodging allowance of £6 10s. a year. This was to be a very brief appointment.

Oct. 13th – Mr Davies was quick to express concern in the log book at the backwardness of many of the pupils in the school, notably in arithmetic. His explanation for this was that 'they must have forgotten very much during their holidays'. Also, the temptations of Stow Fair seem to have been a regular cause of absenteeism. He hoped to improve matters by 'rigorous teaching' and 'very hard work'.[60]

Nov. 10th (Log book) – Mr Davies wrote: 'The very heavy gale of last week has caused much damage all around to the trees and houses. On Friday last, about half past six p.m., my wife was seized with very violent convulsions and was in such a sad state for four hours as to be thought dying. Medical aid was obtained as quickly as possible. She lies in an awful and prostrate condition up to now, and almost unconscious. I have conferred with my managers about this, and they have been very considerate.'[61]

Nov. 14th – The Board agreed to new bye-laws making attendance at school compulsory at age four instead of five, and requiring 'that each scholar shall pass Standard 4 before any exemption shall be claimed'. Whilst the guidelines within the Code indicated that a child of ten should be at Standard 4, in practice this was rarely achieved in village schools. The Admissions Register for Great Rissington at this time indicates that many of those who achieved Standard 4 – and some never did – were aged thirteen, or sometimes twelve and occasionally eleven. A child who passed Standard 4 was able to leave school, but was not required to do so. However, most did leave and probably went straight into employment on local farms.

Dec. 5th – The clerk was instructed to 'request that Mr Davies resign the mastership of the school as early as possible after the next inspection', because his wife had become ill and unfit for school duties.

1891

Mr Davies agreed to resign with effect from March 25th 1891, but his frustration at the shortcomings of the School House were expressed in the log book: 'Doubtless my dear wife's dreadful illness is brought on through cold, and [is] really the result of the wretched internal condition of the uninhabitable house we live in; the outside is made to look decent but the inside, to live in, is most wretched. Bad doors, floors, windows; but one fire grate usable.' Later, he wrote: 'The snow was half way up our front door, and it found its way through the cracks and windows of our old dwelling on to the bed.' On his last day, March 25th, Mr Davies wrote: 'My happy connection with the school ends today and we shall be very glad to get out of our shed into a house.'

Jan. 9th – The Board advertised again in *The Schoolmaster*, but also decided 'to write to the Principal of Culham, Cheltenham and Bristol colleges with a view to obtain the services of a young man'! They subsequently agreed for the first time to invite shortlist candidates for interview prior to appointment. However, only one candidate attended for interview, a Mr G.L. Watts from Uttoxeter. There was reluctance to offer him the job, and the decision was deferred until March. The Board tried to persuade Mr Tennant to return but, when he declined, they concluded that 'Mr Watts be acceptable as master of the school', and offered him the job at a salary of £80 a year. He was later confirmed in his post and his salary increased to £90.

Jan. 16th (Log book) – Mr Davies, who was still in post, wrote: 'Weather exceedingly cold. Rissington roads very dangerous; they are simply one mass of ice to walk on. The weather militates against us. Many sick.'

Three days later he wrote: 'Weather excessively cold, small school. Some unwell. In class I 15 out of 22, in II 9 out of 14, in III 18 out of 30 present. Eva Smith, who 'hates arithmetic', has turned up again this morning. This girl is in an unsatisfactory state in her subjects, especially arithmetic, as also [is] Harry Hemming and Emma Jones.'[62]

June 13th – 'It was resolved that each child shall attend school 36 times per month unless a reasonable excuse be given.' Previously, the minimum requirement had been 30 attendances, which had meant that a child could be absent without explanation for one quarter of the total time that the school was open. Such latitude was common in farming villages, but it made the teacher's job particularly difficult.

Aug. 21st – School fees were abolished under the 1891 Education Act, to be replaced by a Fee Grant from September, thus removing one of the sources of resentment to compulsory school attendance.

1892

Feb. 15th – The annual inspection took place. As usual, the children would have been thoroughly prepared for the visit of HM Inspector; on the day, they would have had to sing songs and recite pieces of poetry by heart, such as those listed below (from the Little Rissington log book):

Poetry – Standards 1 & 2 'A Little Goose'
Standards 3 & 4 'The Wreck of the Hesperus'
Standard 5 'An Order for a Picture'
Standards 6 & 7 'The Merchant of Venice – Act 4, Scene 1, lines 230 to 400'

In other years, the list included old favourites such as 'The Burial of Sir John Moore' (Std. 4), and 'The Inchcape Rock' (Std. 3), whilst those in Standard 2 struggled with 'My Heart's in the Highlands'. 'Mary Queen of Scots', 'Death of De Boune', 'Lochiel's Warning', and 'Loss of the Birkenhead' were regular choices for the older children, in keeping with the spirit of the Victorian era, with poems such as 'Sale of the Pet Lamb' and 'The Woodmouse' being popular choices for the younger children.

List of Songs –   <u>Standards 1-7</u>   <u>Infants</u>
'I Miss them now those Little Feet'   'Robin dear Robin'
'The Rose of Lucerne'   'Poor Peter'
'Over Field and Meadow'   'I'm a Merry Little Soldier'
'Seedtime'   'The Watch'
'The Old Black Cat'
'Good Night'
'This is May'
'Moonlight'

1893

March 30th – As a result of HM Inspector's report, the Board considered it necessary to employ an additional teacher. They later appointed Amy Collett as a monitress, with a view to her becoming a pupil teacher after her next examination. Her salary was to be £5 p.a., increasing by £2 each year until the end of her apprenticeship. The Code required that a pupil teacher receive at least one hour's instruction a day from the headmaster, who might delegate part of this responsibility to a certificated assistant. Around 90% of newly qualified certificated teachers at this time were once pupil teachers.

Sept. 28th – 'Mr Watts being desirous of opening a night school, the Board consented to allow him the use of coals.' The 'evening' school was well attended, and the Inspector's report for 1894 stated that 'good work is being done in this out-of-the-way village, and it is to be hoped that continued and increasing interest will be taken in the evening

Continuation School'[63]. Evening classes were held in the school until the outbreak of the First Word War, and certificates were awarded for aptitude in particular subjects.

Oct. 30th – New members of the School Board included James Mathews, grocer, and Thomas Davis, whose occupation was listed as marine store dealer or licensed hawker.

1894

March 9th – HM Inspector's report stated that the dimensions of the infant room (built in 1877) were less than those recognised by the Education Department. The Board considered removing the north wall to the boundary, thereby enlarging the room by some 12ft. 3in. by 12ft., and agreed to draw up the necessary plans and submit them for approval.

April 27th – The Rev. R.E. Bailey applied to give a Bible lesson in the school twice a week, and this was agreed.

May 11th – The school received a drawings grant of £1 11s. 6d. – In 1890, drawing had become a compulsory subject for boys. The curriculum in elementary schools was now beginning to broaden, following amendments to the government's Code of Regulations and the availability of additional grants for 'specific' subjects, including history, geography and domestic economy. Object lessons designed to stimulate a child's powers of observation and expression had been introduced some years earlier, but now the lists of objects were beginning to include a few topics that were not 'objects'. The diversity of object lessons can be seen from the list below for Little Rissington:

Object Lessons for 1897 – Standards 2 & 3
    The cat, dog, horse, reindeer
    Spring, summer, autumn, winter
    How rain is made
    Local crops (4)
    Birds & plants of the north temperate zone (12)
    The mariner's compass
    Local birds, their eggs and nests (6)
    Linen, cotton thread
    Needles & pins
    Paper
    Measurements of length

Object Lessons – Standard 1 with Infants
    A lead pencil
    Paper
    The cat, dog, horse, reindeer
    A penny
    Bread
    A cup of tea
    The oak
    The Three Bears

The variety of subjects covered at Little Rissington in other years included river basins, industries, roads and canals, The Post Office, 'how we are governed', a coconut, and a garden snail. Whenever possible, teachers would bring examples of the objects into the classroom, perhaps even dissected, for the idea was that the physical objects be seen and handled. Beautifully illustrated books of object lessons were produced for use by teachers, but these would not have been available to pupils in village schools at that time.

June 15th – The plan for the new classroom had been returned by the Department as unsatisfactory. The Board agreed to submit another plan 'to their Lordships providing an additional length of 15ft., thus acquiring sufficient accommodation for 39 children'. It is interesting to see how the Education Department in London concerned itself with the detail of the running of thousands of elementary schools throughout England and Wales – and this was in the days before advent of the telephone. With the increasing expansion of education, it was becoming inevitable that some other form of management and control would be necessary. County and County Borough Councils had been established by the Local Government Act of 1888, and the following year they were empowered to levy a penny rate to aid technical education within their areas, thus establishing a precedent for local authority control in the field of education.

The Holmes family, 1901.
Standing: Annie Victoria, 13; Mary Louisa, 27;
Seated: William Holmes, schoolmaster, 53; Agatha Bailey, 8; Ellen Elizabeth, 49; Reginald John, 11. Altogether, there were eleven children, though one died as a baby, and Alice Emma Holmes died at Great Rissington on 6th March 1900, aged 21.

July 20th – 'The clerk stated that plan number 2 had been returned with several suggested alterations and additions, including a new cloak room. The Board having calculated how barely the whole school premises satisfied the Department and the probability of another outlay at an early date, suggested that a plan of the whole site should be submitted for approval and instructed the clerk, should any further alterations be found necessary, to lay the unsatisfactory matter clearly before their Lordships, soliciting advice as to the best means of procedure.'

Aug. 10th – The Board concluded that 'nothing short of new school premises would prove efficient and permanently satisfy the requirements of the Department'. To add to their overall concerns, they received a letter of resignation from Mr Watts. They therefore advertised again for 'the mastership' of the school.

Aug. 31st – A letter from the Education Department stated that 'their Lordships consider under the circumstances a new school is desirable'.

Sept. 14th – Mr William Holmes, who had trained at St John's College, Battersea from 1867 to 1869, was appointed to the mastership of the school, with his wife to act as a supplementary teacher under Article 68, at a joint salary of £90. His request that his salary be paid monthly, rather than quarterly as had previously been the case, was agreed. Soon after commencing, he began evening classes in the schoolroom. His daughter, Miss Mary Holmes, was later appointed as assistant teacher at a salary of £10 p.a. This was increased to £13 in 1896, but only after she tendered her resignation, subject to withdrawal should the Board 'favourably comply with her application for a rise in salary'.

Nov. 9th – Ground plans for the proposed new school buildings were considered, and Mr Wrigglesworth from the village offered to carry out the architectural work for $2^{1}/_{2}$% of the total cost. A couple of weeks later, the Board considered the plans drawn up by Mr Wrigglesworth for the proposed new school and schoolmaster's house, which were then forwarded to the Education Department for approval.

1895

Feb. 8th – ' The clerk was instructed to write to Mr Holmes respecting certain rumours in the village and to state that the Board could not overlook a recurrence of such practice.' There is no further reference to this incident in subsequent minutes, but it may have been related to Mr Holmes' use of corporal punishment in the classroom. Mr Holmes went on to serve as master for eight years, considerably longer that any other master or mistress of the period. In 1897 he was elected chairman of the Parish Council, which indicates that he was well respected in the village.

April 19th – Approval of the plans had now been received from both the Education Department and the local HM Inspector. 'The clerk was instructed to enquire if E.R. Wingfield Esq. will sell to the Board a piece of land for [the] school site and on what terms. Also, if he will grant permission to dig stone for the proposed new buildings.'

VII

THE BUILDING OF THE NEW SCHOOL

By now, the school building had been condemned as unsuitable; it was too small and apparently insanitary. Classes for the older children were transferred to the Reading Room, while the infants were taught for more than a year in a cottage nearby, owned by Mr Wrigglesworth. Thus there was considerable disruption to school life before the new school building was completed on a site above the village green.

Meanwhile, the Board proceeded with the business of acquiring the land, advertising for tenders and raising the necessary finance. By June 1895, two tenders had been received:

> Mr Wheeler, Abingdon –   £1734
> Hartwell Brothers, Bourton – £1643

Not satisfied, they advertised again, resulting in a revised tender from Mr Wheeler, and one from Mr Clifford of Bourton for £1441 5s. The Board considered such expenditure beyond its reach, and the architect was asked to alter the specification to reduce cost, but his changes only reduced the original cost by £35.

By August, the Board had decided that £800 should be the expense limit for the new premises – this sum now excluded the building of a schoolmaster's house. The architect was asked to prepare new plans within this sum. Mr Wingfield was approached again to see if he would 'grant a piece of land in exchange for the old school site, the Board to be allowed to use all or any portion of the old material in the erection of the new premises and hold the same as the freehold property of the Board, the present Trustee [Henry Rice] having expressed his willingness to renounce all claim on the old premises in favour of the Board.'[64] The new land measured 'one rood and twelve perches' (about 140 ft. by 110 ft.).

By February 1896, new plans had been prepared by Mr Chatters of Knight & Chatters, Cheltenham, who offered to 'carry out the architecture and supervision of works for 5% of the building cost', to which the Board agreed. The plans were then forwarded to the Education Department for approval, but were returned for revision. Once the alterations were made and approved, new tenders were invited by advertising in *The Evesham Journal*, *The Wilts & Gloucestershire Standard*, and *The Oxford Journal*. Three tenders were received and considered:

> Mr Taylor, Kencott –   £1020 4s.
> W. Smith, Rissington –   £787 –
> Clifford & Son, Bourton – £758 10s.

Mr Wingfield agreed to convey to the Board free of cost the new site in exchange for the old one, and William Smith, with the benefit of inside knowledge as clerk to the Board, reduced his tender to £763 10s., which was accepted. The Board now approached the Public Works Loan Board, seeking agreement to borrow £850 'to erect and furnish completely the new school', and to spread the repayments over 35 years. Terms were agreed, and annual repayments were to be £42 10s., at an interest rate of $3\frac{1}{2}\%$ (later reduced to 3%.)

It was at this important juncture in the history of the school that the Rev. Henry Rice died. Like his father before him, he had made a significant financial contribution to the school before it became a Board School. Unlike his father who had been resident in Oddington, Henry and his family lived in the village and took a close personal interest in the life of the school. He did not live to see the completion of the new school.

Henry Rice was succeeded briefly as chairman of the School Board by John Garne, who died early the following year from bronchial pneumonia. Some months after his death, John Garne's renowned herd of Rissington Shorthorns was sold at auction in the village and fetched over £650; 'Countess Pye', described as 'a rich red, with nice head, well set shoulders, nice loins, very wide behind, her tail well set, a good milker and breeder', fetched the highest price at 63 guineas.[65]

On December 4th 1896, the school was closed by order of the Rural District Council until February 22nd owing to the prevalence of scarlet fever. During this closure the newly elected School Board decided to admit the public to all future meetings of the Board.

A building specification for the proposed mixed school at Great Rissington dated 5th August 1896 – in accordance with the drawings prepared by Knight & Chatters – survives, and below is a summary of some of the clauses which throw light on aspects of the school buildings at that time:[66]

– 'Provide and hang plain but strong wrought iron gates to the girls and infants entrance, and to the boys entrance, the latter to be a pair of gates 8ft. wide for cart entrance. The gates to have padlock and chains.
– The exterior facing of the walls to be of local stone, ... the old stone from the present school to be used as far as is suitable. The worked stonework, quoins and all dressings, to be of Farmington stone.[67]
– The floors of entrance lobbies, hat and cloak spaces ... to be paved with 9in. red quarries – best quality – set in cement on a bed of concrete 4in. thick – the ground being made up and firmly rammed.
– Provide and fix hearths to the fireplaces of hard stone, or tiles ... Provide and fix mantle registers in school room and class room – prime cost 40/- each.
– The privy vaults to have 4in. cast iron pipes from the top of same and carried up above the roofs, for ventilation ... Provide stone covering for the vaults, so as to be easily movable for cleaning out – to rest on pieces of *railway rails*.'

There was a further requirement to fix 40 strong wrought iron hat and coat hooks in the boys' lobby, and 80 such hooks in the girls' and infants' lobby. This provides confirmation of the statement in *Kelly's Directory* that the school was built for 120 children, though the average attendance in 1897 was 75.

FORMER PRIVIES AT THE SCHOOL

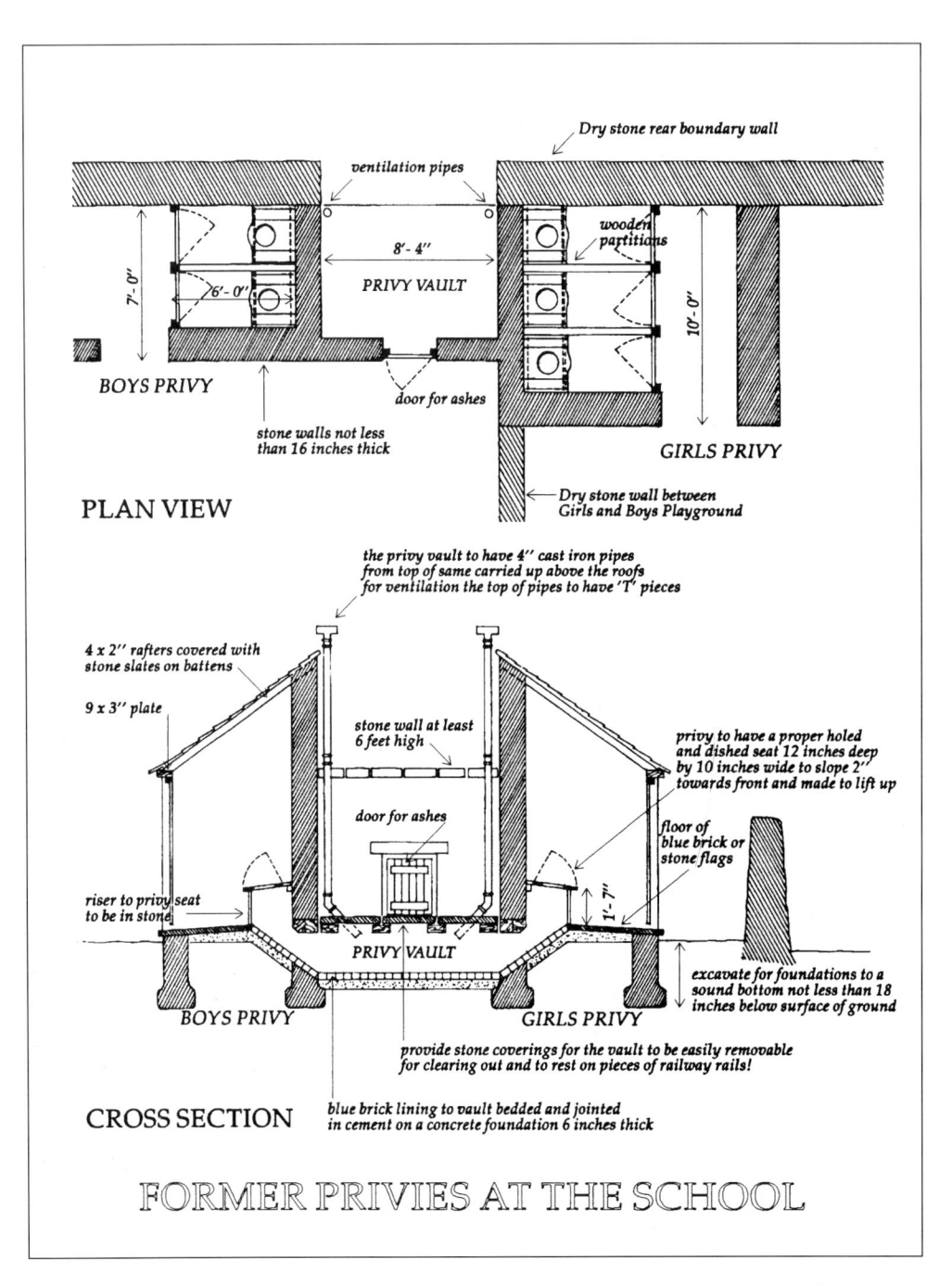

A plan view of the earth closets - or privies - at Great Rissington School, together with a cross-section of a privy vault based on a design for schools by Sylvanus Trevail in 1892 *(PRO, ED 9/21)*. These privies continued in use until 1949.
Drawings by Mike Pennington.

The contract conditions stipulated that the contractor be 'answerable for the stability of the work for 12 months after completion'; also, 'the work to be completely finished by the 1st day of August 1897, and if not so completed, the contractor to pay and allow the sum of three pounds for each and every week the works remain uncompleted after the time named, as liquidated damages'. In the event, the building was completed on time.

As the new school was nearing completion, the village celebrated Queen Victoria's Diamond Jubilee. *The Wilts and Gloucestershire Standard* carried the following report on 26th June:

'The festivities here consisted of a dinner to all the men, and a tea to all the women and children. A general subscription was made throughout the parish and substantial assistance was given by the squire, Mr E. Rhys Wingfield. The rector, the Rev. H. Madan Pratt presided at the dinner and teas and proposed the toasts of "The Queen" and "The Squire". A cricket match was played between married and single. The commemoration services on Sunday were largely attended. The musical portions were exceedingly well rendered, the rector's daughters playing their violins in the National Anthem. The rector preached at both services from Proverbs xxxi. 29 [Many daughters have done virtuously, but thou excellest them all], and Psalm lxvii. 3.'

Some two months earlier, the same paper reported that the children had observed the old May Day custom of carrying May garlands around the village. After assembling at the school, they marched in procession to each house, 'returning at mid-day with a well-filled purse, the proceeds of which were to defray the cost of tea. The afternoon was spent in various games.' A surplus from the morning's collection was divided among the older schoolchildren.

On August 13th 1897, the School Board met in the new school for the first time. The new rector, the Rev. Madan Pratt, had been elected chairman in deference to his learning and position in society. The clerk was instructed to order from the Educational Supply Asociation, 12 desks each 7ft. 6in. long, 4 desks 6ft. long, and 6 windsor chairs. From the numbers at the school, it would seem that four or five children sat at each desk, depending on their age and size. Two additional infant desks were ordered a year later, following HM Inspector's visit. The school furniture and books were insured, the amount being £100 in 1901.

All was now ready for the return of the children after the harvest holidays. A report in *The Wilts and Gloucestershire Standard* described the official opening of the school, which took place on 17th September:[68]

'OPENING OF THE NEW BOARD SCHOOL – This interesting ceremony took place on Friday last, when the order of proceedings was as follows: – 4 p.m., school and choir boys' tea (given by Mrs Pratt); 5 p.m., public tea at 6d. per head; 6 p.m., opening ceremony, carried out by the Rev. H. Madan Pratt, rector and chairman of the School Board, and Mr E.R. Wingfield of Barrington Park; 7 p.m., school children's entertainment. Mrs Pratt provided tea for about 100 children, who

The school, soon after it was rebuilt on a new site above the village green in 1897.
The pole in front of the school has a crown at the top and was probably erected
for the diamond jubilee of Queen Victoria earlier that year.

The school and some of the children in the early years of this century.
Could the man in the picture be Mr T.E. Smith, headmaster from 1907 to 1911?

The family of Edwin Agg, c.1910. *From the left:* Kitty, Mahala Agg, Dorothy Alice (later Duester), Lotte (later Surch), Edwin Agg, Nell

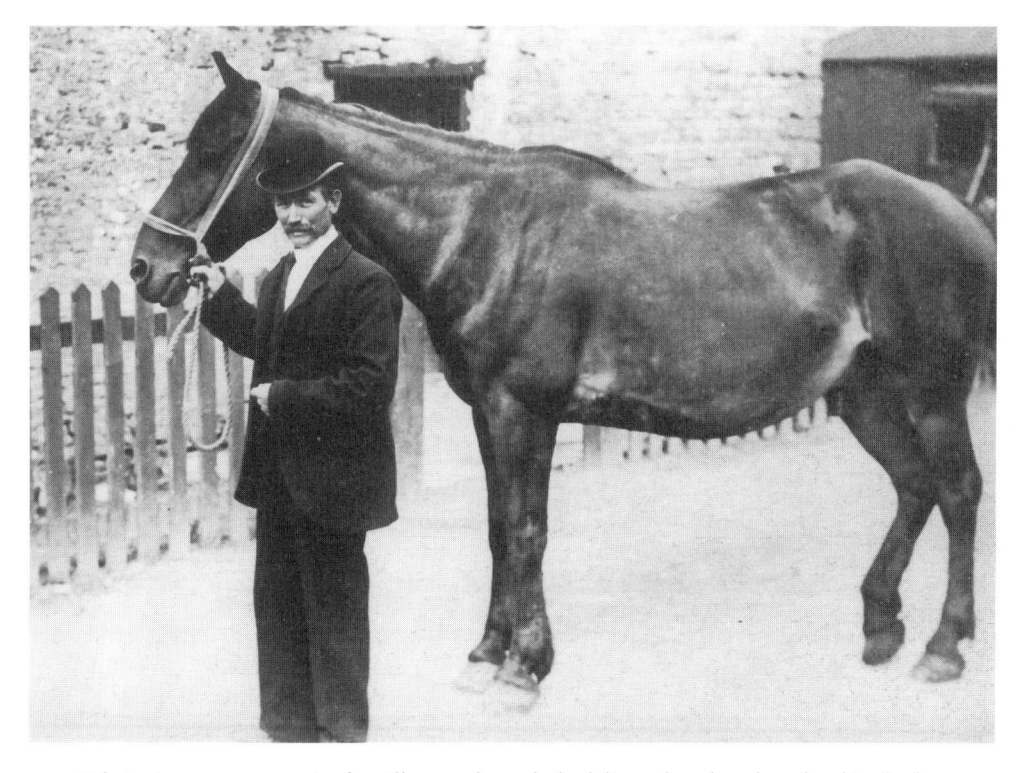

Edwin Agg was a carter in the village and regularly delivered coal to the school in the last decade of the nineteenth century and in the years before the First World War.

were delighted with the good things supplied. They were attended to by the Misses Wingfield and other willing hands. At the five o'clock tea there were about 70 sat down, and they expressed satisfaction to Mrs Holmes, who kindly undertook the providing for them. After the teas, the rector held a short and appropriate service of prayer and thanksgiving, and then Mr Wingfield, in a short but suitable speech, pronounced the school open for the education of this, and he hoped, future generations of children belonging to the parish. Mr W. Smith, the contractor and clerk to the School Board, followed with a few words and made known that the 'squire', Mr Wingfield, had given the land on which the school is built. This announcement was received with much cheering, after which the rector moved a vote of thanks to the squire for his kindly action in coming to open the splendid buildings, and also to Mrs, the Misses, and Mr C. Wingfield and others for their welcome presence. At seven o'clock, the schoolchildren gave an entertainment of songs, plays, recitations, etc., to a crowded audience, and at the close Mr C. Wingfield moved a vote of thanks to Mr Holmes, the schoolmaster, who had, under difficulties, got up such a pleasing evening's amusement.'

The new school opened for lessons on Monday September 20th. There is no mention of any teething problems, although it is obvious from later reports by HM Inspector that the heat provided from the fireplaces was inadequate for the large rooms, despite quantities of fuel supplied each year by Edwin Agg, a carter in the village. Lighting was provided by means of oil lamps – mains electricity did not come to the village until 1937. There were little things to sort out, such as the need to 'provide and fix a washing trough with two bowls in the lobby for use by the girls doing needlework'. There was of course no supply of water on site – all water had to be fetched each day from the nearest well by the village green. It was not until 1926 that standpipes were set up in the village to replace the wells. By 1940, most houses had a piped water supply from a reservoir, and mains water came in 1954.[69]

The years leading up to and following the building of the new school were accompanied by a significant fall in the population of the village (see Appendix 3), which mirrored the decline in the numbers of people working on the land. Between 1871 and 1901, the numbers of males engaged in agriculture in England fell by nearly a third and the number of females by almost 80%. This was partly a result of mechanisation, but was due more to migration and the growth of better paid employment opportunities in the army, police, railways and the Post Office. Another important factor was the growth of dairy farming and a corresponding reduction in the more labour intensive arable farming.[70] A consequence of this was that within a generation of the completion of the new school, numbers would fall to less than thirty.

VIII

THE FINAL YEARS OF THE SCHOOL BOARD

Shortly after the new school had been completed, a former pupil by the name of John Hemming died of 'Lock Jaw' several weeks after being involved in a fight outside 'The Lamb beerhouse'. A report of an inquiry into the cause of death was carried in the *Gloucester Journal* on the 4th September 1897.[71] John Hemming and his brother William, both labourers in Great Rissington, had returned to the village after playing a cricket match in Sherborne. They later went into The Lamb, where John sat down at the bar with several others, including Thomas Stafford who was a carter in the village. A conversation took place between John Hemming and Stafford about work. When the pub cleared at 10 p.m., Hemming and Stafford began quarrelling. 'The men were going to fight, and Hemming said to Stafford, "come out if you are a man".' A fight started, and when William Hemming next saw his brother, he was on the ground face downwards. He was described as being 'not sober, but not very drunk, and able to stand'. He had a broken nose and his forehead was bruised and grazed. His brother said that he had been quarrelsome that night, but slept well. The next day he complained of a stiff neck. Giving evidence, the surgeon at Bourton cottage hospital said that 'death was due to tetanus'.

During the 1890s, a pleasant young curate, the Rev. M. Hume, provided interest for the boys by organising a football team in the winter and cricket in the summer. Through these games, contacts were made with other villages, such as Wyck Rissington and Great Barrington. There were also occasional visits out of school; the older children were taken to see farm machines in use, such as the new three-furrow steam plough and a self-binding reaper. As part of their nature observation, they were also taken to see the planting, pruning and grafting of trees.[72] In most other respects however, school life remained much as it had done before, and problems of bad attendance persisted, making it necessary for the Attendance Officer to issue warnings to parents from time to time.

1899

Jan 14th – 'The clerk was instructed to ask Mr Bamford to discontinue the practice of illegally employing boys attending the school at the annual shooting parties.'

July 14th – There were further cases of irregular attendance, 'owing chiefly to fruit picking and hay making'.

The Return of Schools and Accounts published by the Education Department for the year 1898-99 provides details of the income and expenditure of each school for the year ending 31st August 1899.[73] For Great Rissington, income equalled expenditure, whereas the schools at Little and Wyck Rissington and Great Barrington all spent more than they received. Total annual expenditure per pupil was £1 18s. 6d. at Great Rissington and Great

Barrington, compared to £2 10s. at Little Rissington and £2 16s. 3d. at Wyck Rissington. These differences were significant, with Little Rissington spending some 30% more per pupil than Great Rissington during 1898-99, the major difference being on salaries. The figures below for Great Rissington are based on an average attendance of 68 during the year:

Income	£ s. d.	Expenditure	£ s. d.
Annual grant paid, 1898-9	61 3 6	On salaries of teachers	103 0 0
Fee grant	31 2 6	Books, stationery, furniture	14 17 8
Aid grant	Nil	Fuel, cleaning, repairs, rent etc.	13 3 1
Rates / voluntary contrib.	35 0 11		
(Rates amount per pupil – 10s. 4d.)			
Science & Art Dept.	1 18 0		
From other sources	1 15 10		
Total Income	131 0 9	Total Expenditure	131 0 9

Aug. 11th – The Board was concerned about the level of rates to be levied; after some discussion, they agreed to 'issue a precept on the overseer for the sum of twenty pounds'. Any shortfall in income over expenditure, after taking account of all government grants, had to be made up from local parish rates. It was up to the Board to determine how much they required to cover the shortfall; a precept was normally issued three times a year.

During Christmas week, the Rev. Madan Pratt arranged for an evening party to be held in school, and a jumble sale took place to raise funds. At other times of the year, he organised a bazaar and was generally active in supporting the school.

1900

The school was closed for several weeks in March, 'owing to a great amount of sickness among the children'. It was closed for a further month from early April 'owing to measles in the master's house'.

March 9th – The Board decided to deduct five shillings a month from Mr Holmes' salary after the Education Department deducted £3 a year from the annual grant as a contribution to the Teachers' Superannuation Fund.

Nov. 30th – In response to a letter from the newly created Board of Education referring to the non-attendance of children under fourteen, steps were agreed to enforce the attendance of the named children. In order to try to reduce such problems in the future, the School Board 'resolved that every child eligible be presented for total or partial exemption [from attendance] at any visit by HMI'. And to aid the teaching of music, a second-hand harmonium was purchased for £4. Previously, the children used to sing unaccompanied after an initial note from a tuning-fork.

1901

Jan. 23rd – The rector came to the school to announce the death of Queen Victoria on the previous day. He gave a talk on some of the outstanding events that had occurred during her long reign.

The infant class in 1901, with Mr Holmes, headmaster, and Mary Louisa, assistant teacher.

The junior class in 1901, with Mr Holmes and his wife, Ellen Elizabeth, supplementary teacher.

On a memorable day in the Spring, the older children walked to Bourton-on-the-Water (some three miles each way) to see a small circus; there was also a wild beast show, with animals that none of them had ever seen.[74]

April 12th – Mr Brook, 'in very suitable words alluded to the loss the parish generally had sustained by the death of E.R. Wingfield Esq. of Barrington Park', and a vote of condolence was sent to Mrs Wingfield.

May – Traditional May Day festivities were revived by Mr Holmes, who allowed his garden to be used for dance practice to the accompaniment of a mouth organ. Most of the children wore plimsolls purchased from the village shop.[75] The mood of the nation found expression on Empire Day – May 24th – when the children sang patriotic songs and saluted the Union flag as they marched past. This was the age of imperialism, and military drill formed part of the school curriculum. History and geography textbooks reflected a sense of pride in Britain's vast empire.

July 15th – Mrs Davis resigned as school cleaner after nineteen years' service.

The Rev. Madan Pratt used the *Stow Deanery Magazine* to report all sorts of items of news within the village and his entries give us a valuable insight into the social life of the village at that time. The school was a focal point for meetings and entertainments in the village, and in January 1902, he wrote:[76] 'On Monday evening December 16th [1901], a meeting was held at the school at 7 o' clock. The rector read out a list of [missionary] boxes in the parish and introduced the Rev. E.C. Spicer, who gave a most interesting address on Australia, manipulating a magic lantern himself, the slides being photographs that he had taken himself when in that country. The meeting was well attended. The collections in church and at the meeting, and contents of the boxes amounted to £2 14s.' Later in this edition, he wrote: 'Almanack 1902 – The rector has presented to every house in the parish a localised and beautifully coloured "Fireside" Almanack for 1902.'

1902

The rector commented in the deanery magazine that HM Inspector de Sausmarez had visited the school on February 5th 'and found all in good order'.

The rector continued to chair meetings of the School Board, which met in February to deal with a problem relating to Mr Holmes. 'Owing to rumours which had reached members of the Board relative to the efficiency and conduct of the school staff and the fact that several boys had been taken from the school', it was agreed that the clerk write to Mr Holmes as follows: 'At a meeting of the School Board held Feb. 14th, it was resolved that owing to the apparent unsatisfactory results obtained in the school and from examples to children which the Board does not approve, you are requested to resign your duties as master of the school.'

It seems that the Board members were very ready to act on rumours, and again, there is no evidence that they were investigated or substantiated. Mr Holmes had successfully steered the school through a difficult period, and he was remembered by old pupils in the 1950s as having introduced 'new ideas and far more interesting teaching methods'. He was a respected member of the community, having been elected chairman of the Parish Council five years earlier. Perhaps his new methods or his strict enforcement of discipline met with the disapproval of some parents in a traditional farming village at that time.

In common with other headteachers, he made use of corporal punishment and it seems probable that some parents took exception to this. Mr Holmes duly resigned and went on to become the headmaster of a school at Lyng, near Taunton; this would not have been possible unless the Board had given him a favourable testimonial. Before leaving the village, the rector presented Mr and Mrs Holmes with a dinner service 'in the name of the parents and children attending the school'.[77]

Mr Holmes' daughter, Mary Louisa, was given an excellent reference signed on behalf of the Board by the Rev. Madan Pratt, which said that she had 'given ... entire satisfaction. She is very much beloved by the children, who on her leaving presented her with a handsome present'.[78] The deanery magazine recorded that she was presented with 'a beautiful inkstand and writing case subscribed for by the parents and children of the parish as a token of their esteem and affection for her'.

The Board once more advertised for a certificated master and his wife at a joint salary of £90 'with house and garden'. In April, Mr John Edwards of Birmingham was appointed as master, with his wife to act as a supplementary teacher, and Nellie Agg was appointed as monitress at a salary of £5 p.a. Within a couple of months, Mr Edwards was appointed captain of the newly formed cricket club in the village.

May 2nd – The Board decided to rent for themselves the premises occupied by Mr Holmes on the expiry of his tenancy, at a yearly rent of £10.

Holidays were granted 'for Coronation festivities' on June 25th and 26th, and Squire Wingfield entertained all pupils and parents to tea in the school. Afterwards, games were played and a bonfire was lit when darkness fell.

Oct. 6th (Log book) – Mr Edwards wrote: 'Received a very defiant note today as an excuse for the absence of Cecil Mace on Friday afternoon. Have forwarded the same to the clerk in order that the same may be laid before the Board. The boy has been working in the harvest fields for two half-days last week.'[79]

Nov. 14th – On the advice of HM Inspector, Annie Hemming was appointed as sewing mistress to teach needlework on Monday and Thursday afternoons, at 3s. a week. This appears to have been a temporary apointment, which failed to satisfy the Board of Education. It is interesting to compare her 3s. a week for approximately four hours work with an average of 12s. a week earned by an agricultural labourer in the village in 1912 – or 9s. a week some sixty years earlier.

1903

Feb. 6th – Miss F. Wooley was substituted for Mrs Edwards to act as supplementary teacher under Article 68, at a salary of £15 a year; Mr Edwards' salary was reduced to £75 to reflect this change. At least he was not asked to resign, as had the hapless Mr Davies back in 1890.

The final meeting of the Great Rissington School Board took place on March 23rd 1903. From April 1st, responsibility for the management of the school was assumed by Gloucestershire County Council. William Smith became correspondent for the school, maintaining a link between the newly formed committee of six local managers and the more remote authority.

IX

GREAT RISSINGTON COUNCIL SCHOOL – TO 1920

The Rev. Madan Pratt continued to take a close interest in the school, and writing in the deanery magazine he described an evening of entertainment put on by the children in February 1904:

'A most successful entertainment was given by the children attending the Council School, which reflected the greatest credit on Mr Edwards (master) and the rest of the school staff. The entertainment consisted of school songs, recitations, and drills by the infants, followed by a 'Nigger Entertainment'. A very pretty item was a 'Fan Drill' by twelve girls dressed in Japanese costume, and another item which produced roars of laughter was a dialogue between a recruiting sergeant and a village yokel. The Burlesque Band was a favourite with the audience. All the accompaniments were played by the rector and Miss Pratt. Between the parts, the rector distributed John Webb's charity to the scholars for regular attendance ... '

The annual meeting of the Missionary Society took place in the schoolroom in December 1903, and individual contributions were recorded in the deanery magazine for all to see:

'The meeting opened with prayer and hymn 358, after which the rector read out the contents of the Missionary boxes, viz. : Miss Brook 3s., ... Mrs White (shop) 6s. 2d., Mrs William Smith senior, 3s. 6d., Sarah Annie Bartlett Richings 2s. 5^1/$_2$d., Miss Agatha and Oonah Pratt 9s. 9^1/$_2$d., Sunday and week scholars 1s. 4^1/$_2$d. ... Total sent to the Society, £4 13s. 9d. The Rev. F. Perry, a missionary from Borneo, then gave a most interesting account of the work of the Society in that island, illustrated by magic lantern slides which were certainly the best we have seen. The meeting closed with hymn 220 and prayer.'

A concert took place at the school at 7.30 p.m. on 12th January 1904, and the cost of admission was either 1s., 6d. or 3d. The proceeds (amounting to £3 3s. 6d.) were given to the parish Reading Room. The rector wrote: 'The choir sang (unaccompanied) Mendlessohn's beautiful part song 'Departure' with great taste and feeling. A violin solo, 'Gavotte Mignon' was well played by Miss Dorothy Pratt, accompanied by Miss Pratt. Nearly every item being encored caused the entertainment to last until 11 o' clock.'

The four daughters of the Rev. Madan Pratt with their musical instruments, probably in the early years of this century.

Later that year, the rector, still a major landowner in the village, made arrangements for others to take services in the village church during his absence. He wrote in the deanery magazine that he had 'let The Rectory for a month to the Duke of Leeds for the fishing'.

By now, standards of achievement within the school were improving. An entry in the log book for February 1904 records that Florence Smith, newly promoted to Standard 6, won first prize for an essay on King Canute in a competition open to scholars throughout the British Isles. Two years later, Alice Howse also reached Standard 6 at the age of twelve and obtained her Labour Certificate enabling her to leave school.

Soon after taking over responsibility, the County Council undertook an audit of all school premises. The County Surveyor's report on Great Rissington[80] found, for example, that 'the outside painting is in a very bad state, and apparently has not been done since the school was erected', and 'the playgrounds have a rough gravel surface, and are badly cut up with water courses. They are not properly drained.' The external conveniences (girls and infants, 3 – boys, 2) were said to be in good condition, as were the floors of the school rooms. However, the sides of the fireplaces were described as burnt out, and the ceilings very badly cracked. The colouring on the walls was also 'very bad'. The most serious problem was inadequate heating, which was to cause adverse comment from HM Inspector.

[Labour Certificate form reproduced below]

Labour Certificate for Alice Howse stating that she had reached the 6th Standard, 1906.

On 1st March 1904, HM Inspector's annual report was received:[81]

Mixed School – Average Attendance, 74
'A very considerable improvement has been made during the year in both elementary and class subjects. Arithmetic and music are specially well taught. The arrangement for the teaching of needlework is not at all satisfactory. The probationer should not teach more than half time.
– The school is not sufficiently warmed. Even during this mild winter the temperature of the rooms has been as low as 36°F.' The report recommened that 'additional warming apparatus should be provided before next winter', and that the staff should be strengthened.
Infant Class
– 'There is improvement both in the order and in the quality of work'.

On 11th March 1904, a special report from the Board of Education on Great Rissington School was sent to the Gloucester County Education Committee, requesting to be kept advised on what action the Committee proposed to take 'to place the school in a more satisfactory condition'.[82] The report expressed two main complaints:

– 'I am not satisfied with the way in which the Local Managers perform their duties in the case of this school, and I wish the attention of the Local Education Authority [LEA] called to the matter. The fact that during the past year one of the managers has illegally employed a boy for seven months is sufficient evidence in support of my complaint. This matter has now been dealt with by the LEA. It is however, not the only case of illegal employment at this school.

– On 3rd November 1902, I made an entry in the log book calling attention to the weakness of the teaching staff [under strength], and to the unsatisfactory arrangement made for the instruction of the infants in conjunction with the teaching of needlework. At that time, for two afternoons a week, a class of 28 infants was left in [the] charge of a monitress. She now is recognised as a probationer, but the condition that she shall only work half time is ignored. A sewing mistress who was engaged after my visit in November 1902 was temporarily engaged, but when she left on 30th April 1903 no one was appointed to take her place. A sewing mistress must be permanently engaged, or the teaching staff must be strengthened.'

This report is interesting for several reasons. It shows that, even after the transfer of responsibility to County Councils, the Board of Education in London still became involved in matters of detail within individual schools. And the importance attached to the compulsory subject of needlework is illustrative of the gender stereotyping at a time when women still did not have the vote.

The concept of female domesticity was reinforced by the Board of Education in its influential *Handbook of Suggestions for Teachers* published in 1905. Besides needlework (which occupied 3 hours a week), a course on 'housecraft', including housewifery, laundrywork and cooking, was deemed 'an essential part of every girl's education'. A girl's work in housecraft 'should train her to set a high value on all woman's work in the home', says the 1927 edition; that of 1905 talks of setting a 'high value on the housewife's position'. These housecraft courses were expected to occupy the equivalent of one day a week for at least a year. In the more remote Cotswold villages after 1912, including Great Rissington, a special van visited the school for some four weeks of intensive cookery instruction during the summer months. The *Handbook* also suggested that ordinary subjects such as arithmetic and geography 'often require considerable modification if they are to serve the needs and interests of girls'. And while the girls were doing their needlework, the boys would often be occupied with simple cardboard modelling, drawing, or paper folding.

Returning to the problem of heating, the County Education Committee received a report which investigated the possible installation of a hot water system. This was not thought advisable because 'the apparatus would probably not receive proper attention, as the caretaker is a woman and any leaky joint or small defect would have to be made good by men from Bourton or Burford'.[83] Also, the cost at not less than £200, was considered too high. The removal of the small grate was recommended, with a large slow combustion stove to be supplied, capable of heating the schoolroom (dimensions given as 38ft. by 21ft.).

When HMI Frederick de Sausmarez visited the school on January 16th 1905, he reported that the heating in the Infant's room was defective; 'though a fierce fire was

WADDINGTON AND JACKMAN SERIES.

Punishment Book,

ARRANGED TO MEET THE REQUIREMENTS OF

REVISED INSTRUCTIONS (Appendix II., Sec. 32).

ONE SHILLING AND SIXPENCE.

WADDINGTON & JACKMAN, LTD.

BOLTON : 54, Arkwright Street, and 12, School Hill.
LONDON : 121 and 119, Milkwood Road, Herne Hill.

Extracts from Instructions to H.M. Inspectors, 1900.

REVISED INSTRUCTIONS.

"At your visit to the School you should examine the Log Book, the Punishment Book (see Appendix II., Sec. 32)."

APPENDIX II., SEC. 32.

"A separate book must be kept in which every case of corporal punishment inflicted in the School should be entered."

The title page and instructions from the Great Rissington School punishment book, 1901-1907.
(GRO, S 268/2)

burning in the grate all the afternoon, the temperature never reached 44°F.'[84] Mr de Sausmarez was a well respected and frequent visitor to the village schools in this area. He became an HMI in 1876, and lived in Gloucestershire for more than sixty years. He had won a scholarship to Oxford, reading classics, and later represented the University on the Gloucestershire Education Committee.[85]

The School Attendance Sub-Committee[86]

To deal with poor attendance and the illegal employment of children – problems which persisted right up to the First World War – the County Council formed a sub-committee with responsibility for drawing up and enforcing attendance bye-laws.[87] These required (in 1904) that no child under twelve be employed in any occupation whatsoever during school hours, nor be engaged in street trading after 8 p.m., and that no child under fourteen be allowed into 'any premises licensed for the sale of intoxicating liquor' for the purpose of trading or delivering goods. Whilst the provisions relating to street trading would have had little relevance in a rural community, those relating to the Standard to be achieved before exemption from school was permitted were of considerable importance. The bye-laws for Gloucestershire recognised the rural nature of the county by providing a lower Standard for exemption in country villages than elsewhere. For example, Standard 7 was the exemption standard for Charlton Kings and Stroud, Standard 6 applied in Painswick and Stow-on-the-Wold, while Standard 5 applied in much of the rest of the county. Thus there was official recognition that because of the demands for young agricultural workers in rural areas, few children would progress to secondary education.

Medical problems continued to cause absence from school and in 1908 the sub-committee, on the recommendation of the County Medical Officer, decided 'to exclude all children from school who were suffering from dirty heads'. To prevent this from becoming an excuse for prolonged non-attendance, it was also agreed that the Attendance Officer be instructed 'to take legal proceedings against the parents for the non-attendance of such children at schools', as necessary. This was no idle threat, as a case in Kempsford illustrates: summonses were taken out against a man for the non-attendance of his three children 'owing to their verminous condition', as the parents had previously been fined 15/- and costs for a similar offence.[88]

Discipline and Punishment

One of the main purposes of a public elementary school at this time was 'to form and strengthen the character ... of the children entrusted to it'. *The Handbook of Suggestions for Teachers* exhorted teachers 'by example and influence, aided by the sense of discipline which should pervade the school, to implant in the children habits of industry, self-control, and courageous perseverance in the face of difficulties; they can teach them to reverence what is noble, to be ready for self-sacrifice, and to strive their utmost after purity and truth; they can foster a strong sense of duty and instil in them that consideration and respect for others which must be the foundation of unselfishness and the true basis of all good manners'.[89]

Faced with persistent problems of poor attendance and pressure to ensure that children passed the annual examination in the Standards so that they could leave school, it is not surprising that hard-pressed village school teachers sought to enforce strict discipline. It is possible that they found little time for the noble aims set out in the *Handbook*. 'Dullness' or apparent lack of effort by a child could often result in punishment, as is clear from the Little Rissington log books. Instructions to HM Inspectors in 1900 required that they examine the Punishment Book when they visited a school; all schools had to keep 'a separate book in which every case of corporal punishment inflicted in the school should be entered'.

A Punishment Book for Great Rissington survives for the years 1901 to 1907.[90] During this period, there are some thirteen entries, several of which involve more than one child. The following examples illustrate the variety of misdemeanours which at that time were judged to warrant corporal punishment:

Year	*Name & Age*	*Offence*	*Amount of punishment*
1901	Gilbert Smith, 9	Hurting eye of Ernest Deuster, who gave no provocation. (The fist was used).	2 strokes – one on each hand.
1903	Milly Morris, 10	Crowding in the closets after warning. Result, girl's hat lost.	2 strokes on hand with cane.
1904	Ernest Hitter – James Hyatt, 8	Came to school late. Sheep-driving without parents' consent.	6 strokes on buttocks + 1 on each hand.
1905	W. Edgington, 6	During Oral lesson, made a noise and was asked to come and say why he did it. Did nothing but 'yell loudly'.	Several strokes on buttocks.
1905	James Hyatt, 9	Knocked an apple out [of] a boy's hand and started to eat the same. Briefly a case of theft.	4 strokes on hand and 3 on buttocks.
1906	9 boys aged 7-12	Followed the Heythrop Hounds on Friday p.m. last without obtaining the consent of their parents, and even without going home for dinner. Briefly, 'truancy'.	4 strokes on hand with cane for a previous offender. The rest, 2 strokes on hand.
1907	Boy aged 11	Using disgusting language and throwing mud over the two mistresses outside the school on several occasions after repeated warnings.	4 strokes on hand.

Other offences included 'disobedience and insolence at the same time'. In a separate entry, one child was described as 'a thoroughly bad child in every sense; almost hopeless, not fit to associate with the other children'. It appears that the cane was used sparingly at Great Rissington in the early part of this century.

Health and Fitness

The health and fitness of the nation's children first began to cause concern during the Boer War when significant numbers of men seeking to enlist (mainly from larger towns) were rejected as physically unfit. Many were also rejected due to the loss or decay of too many teeth, and recruits who could not use their teeth to pull a cord through their rifle barrels were discharged.[91] Something had to be done to improve the nation's health and teeth. The government appointed a special committee to look into the problem, and in 1904 the *Report on Physical Deterioration* expressed concern about shortcomings in the nutrition, physique and health of the nation's children. One consequence of this report was that physical training became part of the required curriculum from that year. HM Inspector de Sausmarez recommended in 1911 that '3 periods of 20 minutes each be allotted to physical exercises' at Great Rissington School.

In 1906, the Education (Provision of Meals) Act permitted local education authorities to provide meals for elementary school children, but in Gloucestershire, the Education Committee decided that no such provision was necessary at that time.

Another recommendation of the *Report on Physical Deterioration* was that there should be systematic medical inspection of children at school, and an Act of 1907 compelled LEAs to provide such a service. In Gloucestershire, three doctors were appointed as School Medical Inspectors, assisted by two school nurses, and the first medical inspection of children at Great Rissington School took place in November 1908. One of the first campaigns within the county was to eliminate 'dirty heads' in schools; in 1908, the percentage of infestation was 23.4.[92] At a time when many people could not afford to visit a doctor, it was difficult to ensure that any children identified as needing remedial treatment actually received medical attention. By 1914, the first school dentist began work in Gloucestershire, but most areas of the county did not benefit from this service until after the First World War.

Reports by HM Inspectors, 1906-1910

By 1906, there is evidence of much improvement within the school, although the heating remained a problem. Following his annual visit in January of that year, HMI de Sausmarez issued his summary report:[93]

Mixed Department
– 'This is a very good school indeed. The attendance is exceptionally good, the schemes are well drawn up and the methods adopted are very satisfactory, resulting in general good work. Music, drawing, recitation and physical exercise may be mentioned for special praise.
Infants Division
– The infants are doing very well indeed. Nothing has been done to improve the heating of this room.'

By this time, the school had acquired a piano, generously donated by the Rev. Madan Pratt, and it is clear that it was being put to good use. Besides being used to accompany singing, the piano made possible the introduction of musical drill and games.

A report from HMI de Sausmarez in March 1908 made no mention of the heating, so we may assume that the problem had been resolved by then. His report included the following:

– 'There is desk accommodation for only 24 infants while there were 33 present on the occasion of the visit of inspection, with the prospect of more admissions during spring and summer. The gallery should be removed as it occupies much floor space and its use prevents the work of the children from being properly supervised.
– The use of slates should be entirely discontinued'.

In September 1908, de Sausmarez visited the school again; his observations were:

'1 The teaching especially in the upper Standards of the Mixed Department is vigorous and the order throughout the school is good. It would be an advantage if the junior teachers studied the *Suggestions for Teachers* issued by the Board [of Education]. Simultaneous reading should be discontinued.
2 More reading books should be provided for the infants.
3 The tops of the desks in the main room should be made to slope properly, and suitable desks should be substituted for the gallery in the infant's room.
4 The offices need cleaning and lime-washing.'

The Board of Education was concerned that poorly designed furniture could have a damaging effect, and in its *Suggestions for Teachers*, advised that 'desks influence the posture and attitude of the children for long periods and if too large or too small may tend to produce permanent bodily distortion'. Desks were expected to be the right size for the child, so that there was no need to lean forward at an angle 'with twisted spines and contorted shoulders'. In response to demand, elaborate designs for new desks were produced, including convertible desks that could form adult seats when required – given that most village schools were also available for community use outside school hours.[94]

What was meant by 'vigorous' teaching becomes clearer in the report by Mr de Sausmarez of August 1910:

The children in their Sunday best, 1908.

– 'In a school which cannot be regarded as overstaffed, the teaching is characterised by a vigour which, in itself, is praiseworthy. In order, however, to secure the fullest efficiency, it should be allied with a quieter and more deliberate method. This should involve, in the main, more individual effort on the part of the children, and less actual teaching on the part of the teacher; or perhaps, the concentration of that teaching, from time to time, on a small group, or even on a single child, rather than lecturing to a large class. At the same time it would enable the teacher to pay more attention to essential points which are apt to be lost sight of. For example, the children should be trained to sit in healthy positions as far as possible, though in some cases the unsuitability of the desks may interfere with this. They should be encouraged to hold their pens properly, and the simple exercises suggested may be found useful towards this end. Neatness in the written work should be encouraged, exercises should be carefully corrected – in the presence of the child when possible – and punctuation should be attended to. The practical side of arithmetic should receive actual, and not merely nominal, development, and suitable physical training should be regularly given.'

– 'It ought to be unnecessary to add that the approved time-table should be adhered to, and that the remarks made in previous reports should receive consideration. It is not clear, for example, that the practice of simultaneous reading, though condemned specifically in the 1908 report, has been abandoned. In this connection more reading books are required. Those in use are known almost by heart'.

– 'The teaching of the infants appears satisfactory'.

The maximum number of children to be accommodated at the school was lowered in 1910. Henceforth, the Board of Education determined that the school could accommodate no more than 38 infants in the smaller room and 79 boys and girls in the larger classroom, making a total of 117 (previously 123).[95]

The School House

A new headmaster was appointed in May 1907. The local managers selected Thomas Edward Smith and advised the County of their decision. At the same time, they appointed his daughter Miss Nellie Smith as supplementary teacher 'in the room of Miss Wooley, resigned'. However, the condition of the master's house was causing concern, as 'the landlady, Mrs Randall, is unable to put it in a proper state of repair'. 'As this is the only property available in the village', wrote William Smith, 'I am to enquire if there is a means of solving the difficulty'.[96] The concern was well founded, as we know from earlier log book entries.

In June 1907, the the county surveyor confirmed that the premises – described as being within 50 yards of the school – were in a dilapidated condition. The house was very small, with the largest room being 12ft. 2in. by 9ft. 6in., and 6ft. 10in. high. For this, a rent of £10 a year was paid. Under some pressure, the landlady agreed to undertake some repairs in return for an increase in the annual rent to £12, and the local managers dropped their request for assistance to build a new house.

The School House is the second on the left, opposite the school in the centre of this picture, c.1940.

When the property came up for sale in 1919, William Smith wrote to the Education Committee:

– 'I do not consider the master's house a desirable property to purchase as it is not well arranged and the sanitary conditions are bad, but on the other hand it is the only house in the village that can be got for the purpose, and before it was available we experienced great difficulty in fixing up a master. It would be possible with a few repairs to considerably improve matters.'

The option of building a new house was considered to be too expensive, and the County Architect recommended extensive alterations and additions to the property. It was purchased in May 1919 for the sum of £230, and the rate payable on the house was £1 12s. The School House was retained for the use of the headteacher until 1983, when it was sold by auction for £48,000.[97]

From 1912 to 1914

The year 1912 is noteworthy for a couple of reasons. This was the year that Maud Pratley (now Mrs Maud Pill) came to the school at the age of ten. Now 95, Maud Pill still remembers many interesting details of her schooldays and village life in Great Rissington.[98]

Schoolboys playing on the village green, with The Lamb Inn behind and to the left, in the first decade of the twentieth century.

From the left: Harry Horace Demer, headmaster; Tom Hyatt, pupil teacher; Miss Cambray, infant teacher; Mrs Demer, assistant teacher, 1912.

Maud's father was gamekeeper for the Barrington Park Estate and they lived at 'Barrington Bushes', a house about a mile from Great Rissington School. She used to walk to school each day across the fields, and if it were wet or muddy, her 'button boots' would not keep her feet dry. They had no raincoats in those days and if it rained as they walked to school, they had to sit in class in wet clothes. As an older child, she would sit at the back of the class, furthest away from the stove. The children were not allowed to keep their coats on, and in winter she remembers feeling very cold and shivering for long periods. A bowl of steaming water was kept on top of the stove 'to give a moist atmosphere'.

During playtime, Maud remembers that the girls would often play hopscotch, marbles or skipping, whilst the boys in their separate playground would occupy themselves with football or cricket. From time to time, they had to weed between the stones of the rough playground area. On one occasion, she remembers that Percy Bond, aged about ten, fell and caught his neck on one of the railing spikes on top of the boundary wall; he was apparently badly hurt, and bled a great deal.

In class, Maud sat next to 'her George', George Pill, whom she later married. Each school day would begin with prayers and a hymn. The rector would visit the school regularly, and take Bible classes each week. She and her family went to church on Sundays

The school photo for 1912, with Mr Demer, Miss Cambray, and Mrs Demer on the right.

and when they first came to the village, she recalls that the women sat on one side of the church and the men sat on the other. And if the children met the squire or the rector whilst walking down the village street, the girls were expected to curtsey and the boys to doff their caps. Phil Pratley remembers that his father told him that villagers were also required to acknowledge in this way any members of the families of the squire and rector, and that "there was trouble if you didn't".

The school was an instrument of village discipline in those days, even for matters which happened outside school. Maud recalls the time when some boys broke panes of glass in the village, and their parents had to take the money required for repairs to the schoolmaster.

The headmaster at this time was Harry Horace Demer, whose wife also taught at the school. Maud remembers Mr Demer as a good but very strict teacher, who used the cane frequently. In addition to Mr Demer and his wife, there was Miss Cambray who was the infant teacher, and Tom Hyatt assisted as pupil teacher. Maud recalls that great emphasis was placed on developing good handwriting, though her favourite subjects were history and geography. When the girls were taught needlework, the boys learnt to draw and paint.

It was also around the year 1912 that a special van 'with teachers and equipment for cookery, laundry and housewifery' first visited Great Rissington.[99] The van came for a month in the summer, and was parked in the entrance to a field just above the school. Girls aged 11 and over would receive cooking instruction in the van, about 6 at a time. Maud remembers "making pastries, custards and milk puddings, bacon suet puddings tied up in a muslin cloth, and boiled apple puddings in a basin". She also learnt how to prepare vegetables. "All the cooking was done on a coal burning stove inside the van. Dishes were washed in a sink, and underneath the van there was a large can to catch all the water from the sink, which was emptied each day. Water was fetched by hand from the pump at the village green." Although these vans were also equipped to teach laundry, the emphasis appears to have been heavily on cooking.

By 1912, numbers at the school had begun to fall, though they picked up again the following year. This process of gradual decline in pupils attending the school reflected a fall in the agricultural village population; in the thirty years from 1891 to 1921, the population of the village fell from 419 to 245. The socialist writer and commentator F.E. Green, in his book *The Tyranny of the Countryside*, described a visit he made to Great Rissington in 1912. Green was disturbed by 'the canker of decay eating into village life'. He met the rector, whom he quoted as saying: "Twenty cottages have tumbled down since I became rector sixteen years ago ... But what can we do? The rent is only 1s. 6d. a week, and the squire is a poor man, although he does own three villages. Lloyd George has robbed him of all his superfluous cash."[100]

Green was seeking to make a political point; he paints a picture of decline which, though exaggerated, nevertheless gives an insight into the more general decline in agricultural employment which had been taking place for some years. He described a conversation with a village tradesman who 'spoke bitterly of the decline in the population'. "There is no chance for a man here. The farmers don't keep a sheep to the acre, and but one labourer to the hundred acres. There is a five-hundred acre farm here where only a shepherd, a cowman, a ploughman and one field labourer are kept." Green also spoke to a labourer in the village who told him that 'his wages did not average 12s. a week, taking into account the wet days, and his children had to live chiefly on bread and lard and potatoes'.

The First World War

At the beginning of the war, Mr Higgins was appointed as master in place of Mr Demer, who had left to become head of Sherborne village School.[101] Maud Pill recalls that Mr Higgins was a 'kindly man, always smiling, and quieter than Mr Demer; everyone liked him'. Maud herself left the school in 1916 at the age of fourteen and was chosen by the rector's wife to go into service at The Rectory.

For the year 1914, average school attendance was 65. Every attempt was made to carry on with classes as normal; events such as the Christmas play continued to take place, and the cookery van came for three or four weeks during the summer months as usual. However, there were several ways in which the impact of war was felt within school. The girls were soon involved in knitting and sewing for the soldiers during periods set aside for needlework. By 1915, the girls were likely to have been doing work for the Red Cross during sewing lessons.

The older boys were permitted to work in the fields for long periods at a time to take the places of those who had enlisted, and school attendance fell as a result. At the end of February 1916, a Children's Egg Week was organised to provide eggs for wounded soldiers. The children brought eggs into school, which were packed up and forwarded to various collection depots. Later, in accordance with instructions from the Education Committee in September 1918, children and teachers picked large quantities of blackberries to be used to make jam for the army and navy.

Ernest, Jessie and Grace Hyatt in front of the entrance gates to the boys' playground, c. 1913. Their father, James Hyatt, was the publican at The Swan Inn.

Mr and Mrs George Vellender at their daughter's wedding, c. 1920. Their two sons, both former pupils at the school, were killed in action during the First World War.

The Manor, Great Rissington, probably in the decade before the First World War. An additional wing was added later by the Marlings. On special occasions, the children were entertained at the Manor.

The annual school treat with Mr Higgins, schoolmaster, standing beside the Great Rissington banner, c.1915. Alice Pratley is at the front, second from left.

Everyone was encouraged to grow vegetables at home, as the following advertisement for 1916 in *The Wilts and Gloucestershire Standard* shows: 'It is your duty and it will save you money to grow your own vegetables, they are dear now and will become dearer. The Board of Agriculture impresses upon everyone the necessity of producing as much as they possibly can from their own gardens. ORDER YOUR SEEDS NOW.'

Villages organised whist drives and dances in aid of a fund to provide presents and comforts for the soldiers, and Stow-on-the-Wold set up a Vegetable Production Committee which collected 'packages' of fruit and vegetables for distribution to the fleet. It is likely that Great Rissington would have organised similar fundraising events throughout the war and the venue for these would often have been the school.

School opening and finishing times were brought forward during the autumn and winter months to save coal. At Little Rissington, an extended Christmas holiday was given in 1915 for the same reason, and it is probable that such an arrangement would have also been made at Great Rissington.

Many former pupils joined up to serve their country during the Great War and twelve never returned. Notable amongst those who gave their lives were five sons from the Souls family; this was the highest known loss from one family in any town or village in Britain during the First World War. The first to die was Albert Souls, and a memorial service was held in his honour in the spring of 1916, as described in *The Wilts and Gloucestershire Standard*:

'On Friday evening a memorial service was held in St John the Baptist Church in honour or Mr Albert Souls, the first of our Rissington soldiers to give his life in defence of his King, his country and his native village. The service was very solemn

John Vellender, left, and his brother Fred, dressed up for their sister's wedding outside No. 14 Great Rissington, c.1908.

and made a deep impression upon the full congregation who had assembled in respect for the departed young man. The hymn 'On the resurrection morning' was particularly comforting. The 'Dead March' was also impressively rendered by Mr W. Smith, organist.'

1916, the year of the battle of the Somme, was a sad time for Great Rissington. It is hard to understand today how people must have felt as news of more deaths reached the village. Perhaps the following account can begin to bring home to us something of the sadness of the loss of these young men from the village:[102]

'MEMORIAL SERVICE – On Friday evening July 14th, a service was held in the church ... in memory of John, son of Mr and Mrs George Vellender, who lost his life while fighting in France. The young man belonged to the 8th Gloucester Regiment, and passed away the day before his birthday, when he would have reached the age of twenty. The service was most solemn and impressive and fully attended by the parishioners in sympathy with the bereaved parents. The Rev. H.G. Hensley conducted, assisted by Mr W. Smith and choristers. The 'Dead March' was played while the congregation stood, touched with emotion. The following is a copy of the letter sent to the parents of the young man from the Rev. N.G. Burgis, senior chaplain, Rouen, B.E.F:
– Dear Mrs Vellender, I am so very sorry that I have to write and tell you that your boy Jack died in hospital last night, in the early hours of Tuesday morning, July 3rd. He was brought into hospital a few hours before he died, wounded in the stomach, and it was fairly certain as soon as he was brought in that he could not live. I did not know your son before last night,

but I am one of the chaplains stationed at the hospital and the doctor, after dressing your son's wounds, asked me to go and see him. The boy knew that he was very ill and might not recover, but he died quietly and I do not think he was in much pain. We talked together for a few minutes about life here and life beyond the grave, and he told me that he was ready for either. I spoke to him about his home, and he asked me to tell you that you are not to worry about his wounds and to try not to be unhappy whatever happened to him. I told him that whether he lived or whether he died he would be with God, and he answered that he believed it was so. And so the brave lad died. I am so very sorry for you. But your boy took part in a great fight for freedom and laid down his life in a noble cause. He was buried today (Tuesday) by another chaplain as I left the hospital this morning for duty elsewhere, and his body rests in a beautiful little cemetery with some of his comrades behind the firing line. A cross will be put up later over his grave to mark the spot. I believe Jack told me last night that he had a brother named Fred fighting in Salonica, and I hope that son will be spared to come back at no very distant day. – Believe me, yours sincerely, (Rev.) N.G. Burgis, C.E.'

By August 1916, one month later, another memorial service had been held in the village and another letter had been received by bereaved parents:

'Dear Mrs Porter – It is with very much regret that I write to inform you of the death in action of your son, Private O.J. Porter, No. 13647, at Bazentin, on 31st of last month. Your son was a keen, smart, and a good soldier and very efficient as a machine-gunner, being one of my No. 1's, and was very popular in the section. At the taking of Boiselle, although his gun was blown up and some of his team killed by a shell, and he himself badly bruised and knocked about, yet he continued for two days to carry out his duties in a most satisfactory manner. – Yours sincerely, Edward Pope, Second-Lieutenant MGO, Gloucester Regiment, 8th Brigade.'

In an effort to uphold morale, several open air services were held on the village green during 1916. On 31st May, a Rogation service was held at 8 p.m., 'an hour which allowed the field workers ample time to be home from their tasks and to have tea and a rest, so that they could be present with refreshed spirits. A goodly sight was the assembly of the villagers who had collected in faith to ask God for His blessing on the products of agriculture and all other employments.' On Thursday 10th August, another service was held on the green. The Rev. William White of Bourton-on-the-Water 'addressed the assembly on the general aspect of the times, giving a vivid word sketch of the spiritual and moral forces of the nation, the progress of the war, and the hopes entertained of much good eventually arising therefrom. The subject was entrancing, holding the deep attention of the people throughout. There was a large attendance.'[103]

The Vellender family suffered another blow when Fred was reported missing in Salonica in April 1917; he never returned. His death resulted in the end of the male line of the Vellender family in Great Rissington; although Mr and Mrs George Vellender had eight daughters, their only other son had died in an accident at the age of three.

A full list of former pupils from the school who died in action or later from wounds, is given below:[104]

Children and teachers in 1917, with Mr Higgins in the centre and Mollie White second from the left, standing. Amongst the children are Ruby Bartlett, Harry Mills and Alice Willett.

Name and Rank	Age	Date Killed	Father's Occupation
Thomas Bolter, Private	23	Aug. 1919	Farmer
Fred Masters, Private	23	Sept. 1916	Labourer
Garnet Morris, Lance Cpl.	27	April 1916	Labourer
Oliver Porter, Private	21	July 1916	Labourer
Albert Souls, Private	21	March 1916	Carter, engine driver
Alfred Souls, Private	31	April 1918	ditto
Arthur Souls, Lance Cpl.	31	April 1918	ditto
Fred Souls, Private	32	July 1916	ditto
Walter Souls, Private	24	May 1916	ditto
Fred Vellender, Private	23	April 1917	Cowman
John Vellender, Private	19	July 1916	ditto

The only other person from the parish to be killed during the First World War was not a former pupil; he was the son of the rector, Captain Wilfred Hensley. It is interesting to note that H.A.L. Fisher, when introducing the Education Bill to parliament in 1917, said: "When ... the poor are asked to pour out their blood ... then every just mind begins to realise that the boundaries of citizenship are not determined by wealth, and that the same logic ... points also to an extension of education." "There is a growing sense", he continued, "that the industrial workers of the country are entitled to be considered primarily as citizens and as fit subjects for any form of education from which they are capable of profiteering" *[sic]*.[105]

X

THE YEARS FROM 1920 TO 1937

The Education Act of 1918 abolished all exemptions from the leaving age of fourteen and sought to provide continued part-time compulsory education for those not going on to a secondary school. However, the economic slump and cutbacks in government funds for education meant that this last provision was never implemented. Practical instruction subjects such as dairy work, domestic subjects, handicraft, and gardening could be offered within schools, but the official registers for Great Rissington indicate that such instruction was not offered during the 1920s and 1930s.[106]

By January 1919, Mr Higgins had returned to his post as master of the school; he had joined up in July 1917 and his wife had taken over as headmistress. Mr Higgins, who left in November 1919, is also remembered for teaching a voluntary class of boys swimming and life-saving in the River Windrush. The numbers of children attending school had fallen steadily and by the end of 1921 there were just 41 on the register, with an average attendance of 39 organised into two classes. Numbers remained low throughout the 1920s, falling to an average of just 26 in 1927, before rising to 32 in 1930 and 40 in 1931.

The school received a favourable report from HM Inspector in 1919, who commented:[107]

> – 'This is a good school. The teaching is methodical and effective; the children take an intelligent interest in their work and are making satisfactory progress'. There were however, 'too many weak readers in Standard 1'. The report continued: 'Arithmetic on paper is fairly good, but the oral work in this subject should be better in the two lower classes where tables are weak. The older children are able to solve simple problems connected with their daily life, and succeeded fairly well in working simple tests set them on the day of the inspection.'

Ernest Speller succeeded Mr Higgins as master and by January 1920 was already involved in helping to organise a concert in the school in aid of the football club. The event was a great success and raised £3 12s. 6d. The local paper reported that 'a capital programme was arranged and was well received and appreciated by all present'.[108]

In an effort to overcome criticisms of the narrowness and drabness of education in elementary schools at this time, boxes of library books were sent out to schools in the county after the First World War; the first of these for Great Rissington arrived in 1921. Schools were exhorted to depend less on 'talk and chalk', but rather to encourage children to learn and discover things for themselves, guided by their teachers. Children were entered for external competitions; in the early 1920s Dorothy Agg won a prize for her

The children dressed up to celebrate peace, July 1919,
with Mr Higgins standing, far left, and Mollie White, far right.

Peace celebrations, July 1919. A tea for boys at the school, with Mr Higgins, standing.

Demobilisation for many of those who joined up from the village, 1919. The group includes:
Back row, Arthur Cyphus (3rd left), Bert Pill (3rd rt), Bill Pill (2nd rt)
Middle row: Frank Mills (centre), Charlie White (3rd rt), Percy Lewis (2nd rt)
Kneeling: Mr Higgins – schoolmaster (far left), Charlie Pratley (2nd rt)

Great Rissington football team, including former pupils of the school, 1919-1920.

Children dressed up for a school concert, c.1919.
Mary Smith is the bride, with Harry Mills as the groom.

'fairy-like darning' and prizes were awarded to Sidney Agg and Violet Pill for their illustrated essays on wild birds.[109]

The report by HM Inspector in 1922 acknowledged that 'the number of scholars attending this school has seriously diminished'. The Inspector commented that 'the attainments in arithmetic are not so high', and although work in exercise books was good, 'several children cannot apply their knowledge to the solution of simple problems and failed in a sum set to test accuracy'. Helpful advice was often given by the Inspector, who suggested that in both history and geography, 'sketch maps of the children's own construction might play a larger part in the teaching of both these subjects'. He also observed that 'care has been given to voice production, and the singing is creditable. More attention might be given to reading from note.'

After Mr Higgins left, finding and keeping qualified teachers proved difficult. Ernest Speller resigned as master in December 1922 and was followed briefly by Mary Hockey. Mrs Julia Hurst was appointed headteacher during 1923; she was not a certificated teacher, having failed two subjects in the qualifying examination. In seeking to justify her appointment, the local HM Inspector, Mr L.S. Wood of Cheltenham, wrote: 'The village of Great Rissington has been declining rapidly – I cannot of course say if the low water mark has been reached. There is no squire and, in the present agricultural depression, there seems no likelihood of an increase' [in the village population]. He ends by saying: 'Great Rissington being remote is not an easy school to staff.' He hoped that the Board of Education would sanction Mrs Hurst's appointment.[110]

Children dressed up for the school Christmas concert, December 1921.

By 1925, HM Inspector was able to report that 'music and drawing are commendably taught. The attainments in both these subjects are good and the lessons are thoroughly enjoyed'. He was also able to derive some satisfaction from his observation that the children's work in history and geography was 'supplemented by useful sketch maps, with the result that the older children can visualise the countries they are studying'.

The diversity of employment amongst the parents of pupils at the school had begun to increase by this time. Although there was now greater geographical mobility, only the most well-off families owned a car and many villagers still walked to work each day, sometimes a considerable distance. Opportunities for social mobility were, however, still very limited. In the years from 1925 to 1935 inclusive, the occupations of the fathers of children admitted to the school were as follows:[111]

Labourer	7	Gardener	6
Farmworker	5	Chauffeur	4
Smallholder	2	Butler	2
Clerk/Parish Clerk	3	Farmer	2
Mason	1	Baker	1
Railway Worker	1	Carter	1
Haulier	1	Electrician	1
Innkeeper	1	Shopman	1
Factory Hand	1		

Many families sent three or four children to the school during this period; George Rachael sent nine of his seventeen surviving children to the school between 1925 and 1935.

Albert Pratley driving a Fordson tractor on spade lugs, Manor Farm, c.1930.

The Guides in the stable yard of what is now the Old Rectory, c.1936.
Back row: Joan Smith, The Rev. Frederick Warner, Renee Pratley, Mary E. Lane, Elsie Pill
Front row: Kath Rachael, Irene Rachael, Miss Simmons – Guide leader, Edna Smith

External influences, notably the LEA, played an increasing roll in the management of schools, yet within the village, the influence of squire and rector remained strong for some time. The new owner of Great Rissington Manor – previously known as Manor Farm – was Major William Marling, whose wife soon became a local manager of the school. For many years, she visited the school regularly or arranged entertainments for the children, who were expected to acknowledge her presence if they passed her in the village. The Church continued to exercise considerable influence, with successive rectors acting as chairmen of the local managers of the school and often supporting other activites involving the children. The Rev. Frederick Warner, for example, encouraged the Guides, Cubs and Brownies in the village, who met each week in the stable yard behind what is now the Old Rectory.

The village was still a very close community at this time. Although most people were relatively poor, many kept a couple of pigs and some chickens, and grew vegetables. People helped each other and passed on hand-me-downs. Villagers would meet each other walking down the street or when fetching water from one of the village pumps, and would stop and chat. This everyday social interaction has now disappeared, and with it much of the sense of community that once existed.

During the 1920s, there was a rapid turnover of teaching staff. Not only were there six different headteachers during the decade, but most of the supporting teachers appear to have been either pupil teachers or monitresses. For example, Florence Wallington assisted with Class 2 at the age of fifteen in 1923, and two years later she was listed as assistant teacher for the infants; a year later, she had left. In his report in 1922, HM Inspector commented that 'the young teacher in charge of the infant class has not yet paid visits of observation to an efficient neighbouring school, in order to acquaint herself with modern methods of infant teaching'. In 1926, Florence Blackwell was responsible, as headmistress, for the teaching of all children from the ages of five to fourteen. She was succeeded briefly by Mrs Gladys Gibbs. Stability was restored, and with it a sense of direction, with the appointment of Miss Frances Ethel Grinnell as headmistress in September 1927; she remained as head until August 1946, by which time the school had grown considerably.

The contribution made by Miss Grinnell was soon recognised by HM Inspector, who wrote in his report of 1929: 'This is a school of much promise and the headmistress deserves praise for the sound work she has done since she took charge some two years ago. The tone is particularly good, [and] the attitude of the children towards their work is pleasing ... ' Whilst children in the top group were 'below the usual standard of attainments', the younger children appeared to show more promise. In a later report however, the Inspector commented that Miss Grinnell would be 'still more effective if she planned her work more systematically, and kept records of what she does. In the absence of such records it was not possible to discover why so few written compositions have been attempted so far this term.'[112]

Fred Webb, who started at the school in 1928, remembers that the Inspector's visits "caused a bit of a panic". During his visit, the Inspector would look at the children's work and ask some of them questions to test their understanding. Before his arrival, Miss Grinnell would say to the children, "if any of you let me down, you're in for trouble".[113] The children knew that she meant what she said, for she was very strict and kept a billiard cue as a cane with which to whack the hands of offending pupils.

The infant class, 1937.
Back row: Phil Pratley, Mabel Cambray, Joyce Pratley, Ruby Rachael, Dennis James, Kenny Clark. *Middle row:* Daphne Peachey, Leonard Berry, Vera Smith, Charlie Pratley, Anne Duester, Betty Cambray. *Seated:* Peter Berry, John Rachael, Tina Lester, Pam Bartlett, Helen Peachey, Evelyn Rachael, Peter Bartlett, —

The junior class, 1937.
Back row: Mary E. Lane, Nancy Clarke, Kath Rachael, Edna Smith, Freda Smith, Audrey Pill, Peggy Howse. *Middle row:* Pat Agg, Harry Berry, Eric Rachael, Les Pratley, Fred Webb, Bobby Ayres, Frank Cyphus, Laurie Davies, Arnold Taylor. *Seated:* Joan Clarke, Sheila Pratley, Rosie Rachael, Jean Pill, Florrie Ayres, Ruth Purchase, Marjorie Lewis

How did Great Rissington School compare with other local schools at this time? We have little objective data, but a comment by HM Inspector in his report of 1932 gives a clue: 'the general level achieved [in arithmetic] will now stand comparison with that secured by other schools of a similar type'. However, he went on to say that 'similar progress has not been made in the Literary subjects, yet they are not without their encouraging features'. He also observed that 'handicraft is narrow in scope, and fails to make a sufficient demand upon the constructive abilities of the pupils'.

The only organised sporting activity in school at this time appears to have been rounders, played by both girls and boys in the girls' playground. The boys kicked a football around in their playground during breaks and on one occasion a window was broken. Fred Webb recalls that Miss Grinnell wanted to know who was responsible; no-one owned up and so she whacked them all on the hand, saying that she could now be sure that she had punished the right boy! Other games played during breaks included 'whip and top', marbles, conkers, fox and hounds, hop-scotch, and hoops played with either a wooden or metal hoop and a stick or rod.

The children walked to school and home again without their parents – there was almost no danger from traffic then – and most returned home for lunch. The school day started with a short assembly which included a hymn and a prayer, and the rector came to take assembly once a week. Apart from the three Rs and history and geography, the children learnt to sing, draw and paint. They were also taught country dancing, with Miss Grinnell playing the piano, and physical training usually took place in the main schoolroom. Both girls and boys had to learn to knit – "one plain, one pearl" recalls Arthur Lane. On many Friday afternoons in summer, the older children would go on a nature ramble. School outings were arranged from time to time, and on one occasion the children visited Weston-super-Mare, transported in what Arthur Lane described as "a lorry that had been converted into a bus for the day".

The annual visit of the school dentist during the 1930s is remembered by Jean Pill (now Mrs Ryall) and others, and it appears to have been a fairly traumatic event for many of the children. The smaller classroom became the dentist's surgery for a day or two, where he set up his treadle drill. Children would go in one at a time, whilst lessons continued in the main room next door. Sometimes the yells of children whose teeth were being extracted or treated could be heard, which cannot have helped concentration! Fred Webb remembers teeth being extracted without the use of anaesthetics, which were not normally used by school dentists in the 1930s. Arthur Lane recalls that the only dental treatment most village children received in those days was during the annual visit by the school dentist. During the 1930s, a farm labourer's wages were about 36/- a week and most villagers could not afford to pay for dental treatment.

In an attempt to improve opportunities for secondary education, Gloucestershire increased the number of free places in secondary schools to 40% in 1924, a much higher proportion than for much of the rest of the country. At this time, 'secondary schools' still meant only 'grammar schools'. In 1927, Westwood's Grammar School in Northleach was re-opened after being closed since 1901. But despite this effort to encourage the more able children to try for grammar school places, the great majority of those leaving Great Rissington School during the 1920s and 1930s did not go on to secondary school. In 1927,

The children in fancy dress at the Manor – coronation celebrations, May 1937

The Legion of Honour parade for the coronation of King George VI and Queen Elizabeth, May 1937. Amongst those in the picture are Arthur Cyphus (3rd row, right) and George Rachael M.M.,(5th row, right). Miss Grinnell is towards the back, behind the Scouts and Guides.

none of those leaving went on to secondary school, whilst three boys and one girl left at age fourteen to go into employment; and this pattern was fairly typical until 1945. Amongst those who won places at Westwood's were Oliver White and Lionel Mouser; they were allowed to use their bicycles as transport and were given travelling expenses of £6 a year in 1928.[114] In 1936, John Lane won a scholarship to Westwood's, from where he went on to win a place at Loughborough Technical College. There were other successes at this time, but they were the exceptions.

The school continued to be a focus for entertainments and events in the village, just as it had done in the years before the First World War. Now it was the Marlings at the Manor and the Mitchells at Great Rissington Hill who organised many of the celebrations in the village. For example, a parish tea for about 130 villagers was held in the schoolroom in February 1935 to welcome the new incumbent, the Rev. F.E. Warner. Mrs Helen Marling arranged the event and supplied the tea, assisted by Mrs R.J.H. Mitchell. Tea was followed by 'an excellent entertainment ... by members of the Rissington Glee [unaccompanied part-songs] Party'. Earlier in the month the schoolroom had been the venue for a successful whist drive and dance, with music supplied by Taylor's Dance Orchestra, in aid of the Club Festival Funds.[115]

The occasion of the Jubilee of King George V in May 1935 was an opportunity for thanksgiving and celebration in the village. A service at the church was followed by a cold lunch in the school at which Major Marling, Mr Mitchell and the rector all made speeches. In the afternoon, the children marched from the school to the Manor carrying their Union Jacks, and there they were given tea by Mrs Marling. A social was held in the evening, followed by 'a magnificent display of fireworks' organised by Mr Mitchell.

Two years later, there were great celebrations in the village to mark the coronation of King George VI and Queen Elizabeth. A Legion of Honour parade, which included Scouts, Guides, Cubs and Brownies accompanied by Miss Grinnell, marched to the parish church for a special service. There followed 'a generous luncheon' at the school given by Major Marling for 'all over school age – about 230', served in two sittings with the catering supplied by The Lamb Inn. The tables were beautifully decorated in red, white and blue. There was then a fancy dress procession for the children to Great Rissington Hill, after which they were entertained to tea at the Manor by Mrs Marling. The teachers, Miss Grinnell and Miss Thomas, organised a programme of sports for the children, and each child was given 'a beaker containing a new and an old sixpence' by Mrs Marling. The party dispersed after singing patriotic songs and the National Anthem, and in keeping with a tradition going back at least to Queen Victoria's Diamond Jubilee, a cricket match took place between married and single men in the village. The day's events concluded with 'country dancing and a very jolly social' in the schoolroom, and another spectacular firework display given by Mrs Mitchell.

XI

THE COMING OF THE RAF AND THE SECOND WORLD WAR

As the possibility of another war in Europe increased, an airfield was established at Little Rissington, together with a camp for RAF families and their children. By the end of September 1938, a total of 31 RAF children of various ages had been admitted to the school, and many more followed over the next few months. Some of these RAF children were only at the school for a couple of months or so before they were on the move again. By March 1939, there were 71 pupils on the school register, compared to 41 a year earlier. The school was now divided into three classes; Class 3 for those aged between four and seven had 27 children, Class 2 for those between seven and ten had 22, and Class 1 for those between ten and fourteen also had 22.

Apart fom the presence of RAF children, the war hardly disturbed the daily routine of the school. Early on, the children were issued with gas masks, which they had to practise wearing. Initially, they had to carry them to and from school each day, but this requirement was later relaxed. Mabel Herbert and Anne Grave remember knitting sea boot stockings for the merchant navy, using thick oiled wool which was not very pleasant to handle.[116]

A year after the start of the Second World War, Great Rissington received two evacuee children. Sylvia Fisher from London, a cousin of Marjorie Mills, was admitted to the school in September 1940 and remained for much of the war. George White of St Peter Port, Guernsey, came in November 1940, but left for Folkestone in May 1942. Three other evacuee children also spent brief periods at the school during the last year of the war.

RAF children continued to attend the school throughout the war, causing numbers to fluctuate considerably; by March 1941, there were 54 children on the school roll. In June and July of that year, an epidemic of whooping cough kept many children away from school, with less than a third attending for several weeks in July.

Electric light was installed in the school for the first time in September 1941, by the Western Electric Company. Also that month, Mrs Mitchell invited all the children to the novelty of a cine show at Great Rissington Hill. Teaching continued much as normal, and Anne Deuster and Vera Smith won free places to Westwood's Grammar School. This was also the year that Miss Sayers (later Mrs Walker) started as infant teacher. She remained at the school for more than 30 years.

By now, fundraising was gathering pace to support the war effort and a whist drive took place in the school to raise funds 'to help buy a fighter plane'.[117] A local War Savings Committee was established and they entertained the children in March 1942. Entertainments with a war theme mirrored national campaigns and the following year a

Looking towards the school, right, beyond the village green, c.1938.

'Wings for Victory' party was held for the children; by 1944, the theme for the children's party was 'Salute the Soldier'.[118] Savings certificates were issued to the children, who collected savings stamps worth 6d. each. The government's real objective in these campaigns was to combat inflation and ensure that money was not spent on goods that would use up scarce resources.

The efforts of Mrs Warner, an active manager of the school, and the local War Savings Committee were so successful that the village received praise during a broadcast by the BBC in February 1943. Reviewing the nation's war savings, the announcer said: "The village of Great Rissington in Gloucestershire is not only great in name but great in savings – although it has but two hundred and fifty people. In 1941 they got over £3,000 and in 1942, £7,630. They're now saving at the rate of eight and sixpence a head per week."[119]

The pattern of school holidays was changed in 1942 to allow older children to help out on local farms. The school was closed for a special period of two weeks at the beginning of August, and again for three weeks at the beginning of October for potato picking. This pattern continued for the rest of the war and is reminiscent of the nineteenth century when harvest time determined the start and finish of school holidays. Rupert Duester recalls potato picking at Barrington Park; the children had to pick up the potatoes and put them in sacks or buckets which were then loaded onto a horse-drawn cart. It was hard work and 'certainly no picnic', though they enjoyed being out of school. They had to work quickly, filling the buckets and getting out of the way before a machine came round to dig up the next row. Italian prisoners of war from the prison camp at Northleach also assisted with potato picking in this area. Charlie Pratley, who left school at the age of fourteen in 1944, remembers being allowed out of school when he was thirteen to help in the fields with various tasks including stone picking prior to haymaking, dock pulling in the wheat fields, and mangel pulling (for cattle food in winter). He was paid 3d. an hour for this work.

The position of chairman of the local managers of the school continued to be held by the rector, who at this time was the Rev. Rowan Grice-Hutchinson. Amongst the duties assumed by the chairman, none could be more unusual than the following, as recorded in the managers' minutes for September 1944:[120] 'The chairman reported the condition in which he found the cesspits after they had been uncovered, and as there was a certain amount of risk in carrying out the work of removing the deposit, he had personally carried it out'! The county architect had subsequently 'suggested that the cesspits be filled in and sealed, and that buckets should be used'. On consideration, the managers did not think this feasible and it was agreed that the existing system should be put in order, including the building of concrete removable covers. It was also agreed that the cesspits should be cleared annually, 'which should avoid the difficulties recently experienced'.

The Grice-Hutchinson War Diaries[121]

The new rector, the Rev. (later Canon) Rowan Grice-Hutchinson, was a prolific diarist. We are fortunate to have access to these contemporary writings which give us additional information on life in the village during the war years. It is clear from his writings that the rector played an active part in the life of the village, though it seems that he was never entirely at home in Great Rissington. He took up his duties as rector on his fifty-fifth birthday, June 29th 1940.

The new rector's first impressions of the village were mostly favourable, as the following entries show;

Sunday July 7th 1940 – 'Sunday School in church at 2.30. This is excellent, all most capably arranged by Mrs Warner. Equipment of every description. I opened school but did not teach.'

July 15th 1940 – 'I went out on my first afternoon's visiting and found the people I went to see most agreeable.' Throughout his years in the village, he visited people in their homes regularly.

August 28th 1940 – 'I went to tea with the servants [at Great Rissington Hill]. They had a really beautifully furnished servants' hall and we had a magnificent tea. All was most agreeable. There is a butler, lady's maid, a jolly cook and three young girls from the village.'

Initially, the rector had time to indulge in one of his favourite country pastimes, shooting. However, the practical realities of war were soon being felt:

August 26th 1940 – 'Drove to Great Barrington to see how they had managed the black-out [of the church] ... It must take a tremendous lot of material and be very expensive. Mrs Wingfield gave it, so we could not find out how much it cost.' (From a later entry, we learn that the PCC decided not to black out Great Rissington Church, and evensong was brought forward to 3.30 p.m. in the winter months).

Sept. 5th 1940 – 'I had to rise at 4.30 and go on duty with Mills [Special Constable] at five. There was considerable German activity during the night which I heard ... and once heavy bombs were dropped in the early hours of the morning which shook the house, the first I have heard here.'

Great Rissington Home Guard, 1940-41.
Back row: J. Cambray, H. Pratley, A. Lane, F. Webb, J. Alexander, J. Geden, Rev. R. Grice-Hutchinson, W.G. Clifford. *Seated:* F. James, A. Taylor, Cpl. R. Purchase, Sgt. H. Lane, Sgt. N. Tyrer, Cpl. P. Wallington, H. Mills, J.G. Hunt

On September 11th, the rector went out shooting and the party shot 'a brace of pheasants, a snipe and a dozen rabbits'. During the early part of the war, he was able to go shooting once or twice a week, sometimes at Barrington Park.

Oct. 8th 1940 – 'I went to the gravel pits and got sand for fire buckets in case of incendiary bombs.'

Meetings of the Home Guard took place at the school, which was also the venue for various other lectures on aspects of the war. The rector volunteered for the Home Guard to set a good example, but he soon found the lack of activity rather tedious. Before he was called up, Fred Webb joined the Home Guard and remembers that when the rector volunteered for duty, he was thanked and told that the services of a chaplain would be welcome. Fred recalls that the rector said: "Never mind being chaplain, give me a rifle so that if the Germans come, I can have a go at them!" Fred described the rector as "a big strong man. He was the only man in the Home Guard section who could lift a .303 rifle up over his head with one arm out straight, holding the rifle by the end of the barrel."

Nov. 8th 1940 – 'I had to go to the school and put up the black out ... ready for the Home Guard to which I went at 7.30.'

Dec. 13th 1940 – 'Home Guard at eight at the school. Now I can do the simple drill I quite enjoy it.'

Jan. 9th 1941 – 'I went to a party at the school given to the children by the Women's Institute. It consisted of plays etc. by the children (very fairly done), a [Christmas] Tree and tea ... After tea I ... went to the Home Guard at the school at 7.0. The attendance has now dropped to rather more than half which is rather sad and all the more so since I cannot help feeling that the threat of invasion is becoming more acute. I cannot see how Hitler can keep his vast war machine doing nothing, and I am sure that all these months of waiting mean that he is preparing and constructing and planning and building up in every conceivable way.'

Dec. 19th 1941 – '... went to the Home Guard. I am afraid the latter now simply bores me beyond words. We do much the same over and over and over again with so very much time wasted in various ways.'

March 31st 1942 – 'I ... then went to a very tiresome meeting at the school ... Parishioners [were] to be addressed by the Sergeant of police on matters connected with national defence. But there was scarcely a dozen people there and most of these the old regulars. We did not hear much that we have not heard before.'

June 4th 1942 – 'There was an excellent display of military education films at eight at the school, one on gas and one illustrating an attack by a platoon. Mainly for Home Guard but only grown-ups were invited. Needless to say there was a wretched attendance.'

July 21st 1942 – 'After supper we had to go to the school for a village meeting with two speakers addressing [us] on invasion. There was quite a good attendance.'

July 28th 1942 – 'I had to go up to the school and then make ready for a demonstration of field cookery on improvised ovens given in the afternoon. I worked like a black, assisted by some boys, levelling ground (which is pure rock) in the playground, getting large quantities of (?)earth from the roadside near the quarry (an awful task as all had to be picked out and riddled from the stones) and getting all sorts of things like wood and buckets and bricks for the construction. However, all was ready when the ladies arrived and they seemed very pleased to find it so well prepared. A fairly good concourse of villagers came to see and hear and read and learn and inwardly digest. The ovens are primarily for the Rest Centre[122] but who knows whether a shortage of coal might force us to use them ourselves? And they are very efficient. After tea I finished a second desk for the school. And I wrote a whole sermon after dinner ... The war news, if possible, more dismal than ever. The Russians seem to be going like mad the wrong way and our attack in Egypt appears to have been stopped.'

July 31st 1942 – 'Venables came over at 10.0 and inspected the school in religious knowledge ... Home Guard at night when we did practically nothing except receive a little further equipment. Such a dreadful waste of time.'

Oct. 28th 1942 – 'A lecture on all the affairs connected with the blitz falling on Rissington at 7.0 given by [a] sergeant. There was a meagre attendance. The lecture was quite good. All seems very fully prepared now. What a different position today is from three years ago when all we had was a lecture on gas!'

Wednesday June 30th 1943 – 'There was Home Guard at eight instead of Friday. The gas chamber came and we all went in there to have our gas masks tested.'

July 1st 1943 – 'I went to a Home Guard exercise at Bourton where we did a defence exercise in the open. It was quite good.'

Sept. 16th 1943 – 'A meeting at the school to hear a talk on recent air raids on the E. coast and the new types of bombs used by the Germans. A very pleasant gentleman came from Bourton and it was quite interesting even if it got us very little further. The usual desultory discussion followed which showed the weakness and lack of organisation in ARP

[Air Raid Protection] here. The fact is, as the speaker told us, enthusiasm has waned to so great an extent that now nothing is being done at all in the country – or scarcely anything.'

Mr Grice-Hutchinson was chairman of the managers of the school and his diaries contain a number of references to the school or the children. Initially, his impressions were favourable, but they became less so over time.

Oct. 20th 1940 – 'Sunday School at 2.30 and I took Helen's class as she is away. Quite nice children but they don't know much. None of the boys there. That is the lamentable feature of this Sunday School and partly due, I expect, to its being taught throughout by women.'

Dec. 19th 1941 – 'A children's party in the school at 4.30 when an excellent tea (for war time) was provided by some magic. It was quite pleasant.'

March 9th 1942 – 'A lot of children came at 6.0 and we had a very good evening singing. The evenings are light now and I don't quite know how long to keep it up. They all want to go on but I shan't when there is work to be done in the garden. The (?)dozen boys came as usual. They are very pleasant and keen but deplorably dull. They know next to no arithmetic which is certainly a handicap.'

May 23rd 1942 – 'It was rather a threatening morning with a falling glass but rather a high cold wind ... I went out and finished hand weeding part of the kitchen garden where we have the main crop of potatoes ... Then I got ready, not without misgivings, for a children's picnic postponed from last Saturday, and I went up to Horsehill Lane at 2.30 and we set forth for Dodd's Mill. Alas! It began to spot with rain and we took shelter under a corn stack in the middle of a field. I waited there an hour but it got worse and worse and so we had to go back home. I was only thankful I had resisted the importunities of the children to take a chance and go, for we should have had a fearsome walk home. It rained in real earnest later.'

June 6th 1942 – 'After lunch I took the children to the long planned picnic at Dodd's Mill. We were quite a party and I have seldom known a hotter day. I had been rather perturbed as to what to do with them, but there was no need to be for all they wanted to do was to wade about in the water the whole time. However, we had some games after tea and then came home. All had gone off beautifully and there was nothing to mar the afternoon at all.'

July 16th 1942 – 'I had to go to Bourton after lunch to see [the correspondent] about the school for we have not had a Managers' meeting since goodness knows when and he said he was just going to call one ... I wish with all my heart I did not have to have anything to do with it. And there is the scripture examination to arrange and I know the children are taught next to nothing about it.' The Managers' meeting took place on July 23rd, and concerns were expressed about the school based on unsubstantiated comments from some parents; the rector noted down that he 'suggested that we get HMI to come along and that appears to be the wisest course'

July 27th 1942 – 'I finished off one school table and got the other glued ... to put together when the glue has set.' Later in this entry, he wrote: 'I carried the table up to the school ... '

Nov. 17th 1942 – 'The arithmetic children came at 6.0 and the Sunday School teacher at 7.0.' It is clear from his diary that the rector taught several children remedial arithmetic once a week for a couple of years or more.

Nov. 18th 1942 – 'I am busy writing a little play for the children to act and ... [the choirmaster] came in to help me write it and make suggestions.'

March 14th 1943 – 'There were nearly fifty children at Sunday School – may it continue so.'

June 26th 1943 – 'After lunch I took the children out for a picnic. We went to a field of Mrs Mitchell's by way of the path to Little Rissington. I have never been along it. It is very attractive country. About 35 children came ... and Miss Grinnell. We had tea and they played a game of Indians ... thank goodness, they never seem to tire. We got home in good time. I went up to the dance at the school after dinner ... for the blind.'

Sept. 18th 1943 – 'I took 20 or so children on a picnic at Dodd's Mill. It was quite successful but I begin to find these offices something of a trial.'

Wednesday Dec. 22nd 1943 – 'Church at 3.30 and I went to a party for the children at the school after, which bored me to tears. Just the same as usual and the children disorderly and noisy as they always are here. After supper some young people came here and we practised carols to sing round the village on Christmas Eve. We had quite a good practice and Mrs Vine had typed out seven or eight, and a dozen copies of each.'

Church services were held in the school for several weeks during late November and early December 1943. Although the Reading Room was considered, the rector preferred the school because it was in a more central location in the village. November 27th 1943 – 'I ... got everything from the church and took it up to the school and got it ready with the help of the children.'

It is clear that the rector worked hard to support various activities and committees to aid the war effort. On 9th April 1942, for example, he attended 'a committee meeting of the Food Club at 8.0', which amongst other things had to deal with village entertainments at a time of food rationing.

July 15th 1942 – 'I went out and saw all the allotment holders who belong to the Food Club to tell them that an expert is coming tomorrow to look round. They seemed quite agreeable. [A parishioner's] daughter in great trouble because no-one will buy tame rabbits to eat! and she has gone into it with the greatest enthusiasm. The butchers simply can't sell them – a real blow.'

Feb. 26th 1943 – There was '... a lantern lecture for our annual meeting of the Food Club. Alas! there was a wretched attendance – like everything else. The lecture was admirable and would have been of the greatest possible help for anybody with a garden.'

Fundraising activities took place throughout the war:

March 26th 1942 – 'I went to Bourton and saw the Bank Manager about putting some money in this Warship Week. He told me that if I paid £28 odd for a life insurance policy it would produce £500 towards the funds. So I did.' Within the village, Mrs Warner was busy collecting for this fund, and during the week the local total reached £5,250 which, he comments, led local people to think that there was 'a lot of money about, obviously hinting that it comes out of the overflowing pockets of a few rich people'. He records that 'London has received over £125,000,000'.

Sept. 12th 1942 – '... I had to go over to the Manor and rake a part of a field which had been mown in preparation for a children's sports in the afternoon. This in connection with the Tanks' Drive [to raise money].'

Oct. 11th 1943 – 'Mrs Warner said that already 25 [savings] certificates had come in for the D.B.7 which seems that we shall have upwards of £20 to hand when the end of the year comes. Our quota is £11.' (We know from the school log book that Mrs Warner regularly collected savings certificates from children at the school).

The war greatly accelerated inflation, as the following brief extract illustrates:

April 16th 1942 – '... The budget came out and there is another 2d. on beer which makes it 1/- a pint! ... Money nowadays is like counters.'

Food and petrol rationing created additional work:

May 30th 1942 – 'I did really a tremendous day's work. We sticked three rows of peas in the morning and I did various other things. After lunch I mowed and it took me over two hours ... I have petrol for two or three more times and it will be weary work after that. After tea I sowed the whole of the big flower bed with rows of carrots.'

June 4th 1942 – 'I visited this afternoon and was sorry to find that [a parishioner] is not so well ... The doctor has been and he must go back to hospital at Oxford on Thursday. I wrote to the Petrol Office to ask them to let me have two gallons as a taxi would cost [them] 25/-. I hope I am successful.'

Oct. 18th 1943 – 'After tea I bicycled to Little Rissington and took the lantern over for a [slide] lecture I am to give on Wednesday. No small feat on a bicycle, as it is very heavy and cumbersome.'

In October 1943, an RAF Wellington bomber crashed into the back garden of The Lamb Inn, only a few hundred yards from the school. It had been on its final approach to the runway at Little Rissington, and five of the aircrew were killed. The only survivor was the rear gunner, who was pulled from the wreckage by Special Constable Bert Mills, a former pupil at the school. Mr Mills received an award for 'meritorious services' for his work that night. The next morning children were able to see the wreckage on their way to school, but lessons continued as normal. The rector recorded the event in his diary:

'Oct. 8th 1943 – I was awakened at about two by a crash followed by the explosion of machine gun bullets. I saw a great glare at the top of the village so I went up and found that a bomber had crashed in the orchard just outside The Lamb. How on earth it missed the houses is simply past understanding. One of the crew somehow escaped. The rest of the poor fellows lost their lives. There were a lot of people there and squads from the RAF so I did not stay long and went back to a very troubled slumber.'

The rector was a keen observer of how the war was progressing, and he made extensive entries in his diary. During the Battle of Britain, he wrote daily of the number of German planes shot down, and later in the war he recorded the advances of the Allied armies on all fronts. It is beyond the scope of this book to record many of these entries, but contemporary writings on the progress of the war are rare and give an insight into the context of people's lives during the long years of war.

May 31st 1942 – 'The war news [is] of a terrific air raid over Cologne and the Ruhr. Over 1000 bombers went out and many fighters. It seems truly terrible and I suppose it is only the beginning. May God soon bring this dreadful affair to an end.'

June 22nd 1942 – 'I had a truly wretched night ... I cannot put our disasters out of one's mind ... ' (here he was referring to the fall of Tobruk and 25,000 prisoners taken by the Germans).

July 30th 1942 – 'Poor Cheltenham was rather badly bombed again the day before yesterday and 11 people were killed. Four bombs were also dropped on the aerodrome at Moreton.'

We know that the rector visited the school on D Day, and it is probable that he talked to the children about the momentous events unfolding that day:

June 6th 1944 – 'The great day – D Day as it is called, is come. Our armies have landed this morning on the coast of Normandy, between Le Havre and Cherbourg. Tonight we can only say that the opposition was not so great as had been anticipated. Caen, ten miles inland, has been reached. I cannot write more down. Some day it will be in the history books. May God watch over our men and help us and them bring this dreadful business to a speedy and victorious end. It is too awful to think of.' And later that day he wrote: 'The P.M. made two statements today in the H. of C. He said that our losses had been very greatly less than had been anticipated. The King spoke at 9.0 and [made] a really noble appeal for the prayers of the nation.'

June 7th 1944 – 'Rather a cold day. The wind still blowing but it all calmed down towards evening, so that the Channel should be smooth. There was no further definite news during the day. The lack of German opposition, especially from the air, is very odd to say the least of it. There are all sorts of rumours from German sources, of landings or attempted landings in the Channel Islands, on the west side of the Cotentin and even at Rouen. Pétain has ordered all Frenchman to co-operate against the "Anglo-Saxon invaders". I went to Gloucester to a very important meeting of the Diocesan Education Committee to discuss the appointment of a Director of Religious Education for the Diocese.'

There is no doubt that the destruction and loss of life caused by the war troubled the rector, but the small number of villagers attending church each week, and especially at Christmas, was of particular concern. The following extracts illustrate both of these themes:

Dec. 21st 1943 – 'I went ... to a really marvellous party at Helen's at 4.30 for tenants, work people and some others. There were 78 people there. Would that I could get that for a congregation! There was a tree, a conjurer and presents for everybody. And such a tea as one would not have thought possible in war time. We were not done till eight. So home to write a sermon for Christmas. Alas! ... The principal war news [is] of another terrific raid on Germany. Two thousand tons of bombs were dropped on Frankfurt and another place. Fifty-two bombers were lost. It is really terrible beyond words.'

By the end of 1944, the rector was looking forward to moving on to a new parish:

Christmas Day, 1944 – 'The morning service at 11.0 was dismal beyond words. I never could have imagined so meagre a congregation on Christmas morning. I feel so thankful that, please God, this is the last time I shall be so worried about who comes to church on a great festival and who does not.'

Feb. 20th 1945 – 'So ends this volume. Please God the war in Europe will be over before another one closes. And please God too that we shall find happiness in our new home and, if it be not selfish, that I may get what I have hardly had – peace of mind.'

Mr Grice-Hutchinson is remembered by Anne Grave as a kind person whom she liked. Fred Webb recalls that he was "a lovely man, very charming and easy to talk to. He was a hard grafter, but on his days off, he used to enjoy a pint or two with those who worked for him. He was not a 'yes man' for the upper crust, he was a man for the working class and he was very popular with the villagers. The night before I was called up, he said to me, "I'm not pushing religion at you, but you might like to read this". He gave me a pocket edition of the New Testament which I carried with me all through the war." Phil and Sheila Pratley remember going on bicycle rides with the rector to Guiting Power and other villages. It is clear that the rector was genuinely concerned for the well-being of villagers and every week he visited parishioners in their homes. He worked tirelessly on various war committees in the village and he led by example; if there were something unpleasant to be done, he got on and did the task himself. Any worries that he had, he kept to himself. It comes as a surprise to those who remember him that he was not happy in his ministry in the village.

As the war in Europe ended, the school closed for two days of national holiday on May 8th and 9th, after an assembly and Thanksgiving. When the General Election was called on July 5th, the school became the village polling station and was closed for the day. Later that month, Mrs Marling invited all the children to a celebration party at the Manor. It was to be more than a year before the children's gas masks were finally collected up and taken away.

The Education Act, 1944

In 1941, Winston Churchill appointed R.A. Butler as President of the Board of Education, and told him to 'tell the children that Wolfe won Quebec'. Butler replied that he could not influence school curricula in this way, to which Churchill responded, 'of course not by instruction or order but by suggestion'.[123] This exchange foreshadowed the assumption of much greater control over education by central government; under the 1944 Act, the Minister of Education was made responsible for the education of the people of England and Wales, and the LEAs were required to carry out their duties under his control and direction. The movement of half a million children evacuated during 1940 had revealed just how variable was the provision of education from one area to another.

The 1944 Act envisaged education to be a continuous process for the first time, with three progressive stages of Primary (no longer 'elementary'), Secondary and Further Education. There was to be free secondary education for all, and the school leaving age was to be raised to fifteen by 1947, with provision for it to be raised to sixteen as soon as it became practicable. The Act also made provision for a system of part-time education for all young persons up to the age of eighteen who were not in full-time education.

In all schools, there was now to be a statutory requirement that the day should begin with collective worship and that religious instruction should be given, though parental freedom to withdraw a child was maintained. A duty was placed on Local Education Authorities to provide both milk and a 'substantial' mid-day meal; initially, milk was to be charged at $\frac{1}{2}$d. for a third of a pint (from 1946, milk was supplied free), and the charge for dinners could not exceed the cost of the food. There was also a duty on LEAs to secure 'adequate facilities for recreation and social and physical training'. Subsequent Regulations stipulated that the maximum class size for a primary school was 40, and for a secondary school, 30. Once the supply of teachers and school accommodation increased after the war, the intention was that the primary school figure would be reduced.

XII

THE SCHOOL FROM 1945 TO 1958

By July 1945, the Rev. Richard Wells was chairman of the managers and the possible closure of the school was soon on the agenda. The managers were notified of a proposal to close Great Rissington School as part of the County Education Committee's Development Plan. The views of parents were sought and the managers expressed their concern, but in view of the growing numbers of RAF children at the school, no further action was taken by the county authorities until 1955.

In August 1946, Miss Grinnell resigned as headteacher after nineteen years, considerably longer than any other head of Great Rissington School before her. She is remembered as a good teacher and was liked by some who considered her to have a 'soft heart' beneath her strictness, but others feared her.

Miss Grinnell was succeeded by Florence Joynes, who remained as headteacher for seven years until her retirement in July 1953. There were still many RAF children at the school, and early in February 1947 a case of meningitis at the Camp resulted in all the RAF children being quarantined for two weeks. Later that month heavy snow prevented the bus getting through from the aerodrome for some two weeks.

There were now 66 children on the register, organised into two classes, but initially there were insufficient desks and chairs for all the pupils. Class 1 had 36 children from Standard 2 to Standard 7, and Class 2 had 30 infants plus children in Standard 1. It is interesting to note that the system of Standards which was first established in the 1860s, was still in use at this time, although of course much modified. Practical instruction in gardening was now offered, supervised by an external gardening organiser who 'inspected the gardens at the School House, and brought sets of tools'. On another occasion, he gave a 'demonstration in preparing and planting black and white currant bushes', and expressed satisfaction with the work that had been done.

Headteachers in Gloucestershire were given considerable freedom to decide on their own curriculum and methods of instruction. While a firm grasp of the three Rs was still required, each child was also expected to be able to express himself clearly in writing and speech, and be able to paint and construct. Children were expected to develop their 'physical powers, to take an observant and intelligent interest in their environment, and to learn to live agreeably with other people'.[124] To widen their interests, a variety of day trips were organised for pupils and parents to places such as Windsor and Runnymede by rail and steamer, Whipsnade Zoo, Slimbridge, the House of Commons and the Royal Mews, and Hampton Court Palace.

The rector continued to be closely involved in the life of the school. In addition to being chairman of the managers and coming in to 'give his weekly talk' and Bible lesson,

School outing to Slimbridge, c.1955. Standing at the back, from the right, are: Mrs Walker, Michael Lake, Ruby Hunt, Olive Russell, Florrie Sambell, and Winnie Pill.

the Rev. Richard Horton organised cricket matches for the boys. Sometimes he would give a lantern show of Indian life and hospital work. He also took two boys, Rupert Duester and Charlie Surch, on 'an educational visit' to Oxford for the day, which seems to have consisted largely of watching cricket and learning the finer points of the game.

In the early years after the war, the leaving age for those children who successfully passed the examinations for Westwood's Grammar School was eleven, whereas those going to Bourton County Council (all age) School stayed on until age thirteen. By May 1952, all children left Great Rissington at age eleven, and the school was officially recognised as a 'Junior Mixed and Infants School'.[125] The secondary modern school at Bourton was not completed until 1958.

To comply with the requirement to provide a substantial mid-day meal, a kitchen was built on to the back of the school. Building blocks were delivered and stacked in the 'boy's yard' in February 1947. Kitchen equipment and furniture arrived in April and had to be stored at the end of the main classroom, and the kitchen was not finally completed for another year. A cook and an assistant were appointed, and the first canteen meals were served to '50 scholars' and two teachers on 20th April 1948. By November, meals were also being supplied to Little Rissington School. The headteacher noted in the log book that canteen organisation and clerical work were occupying her to a great extent, to the detriment of her class teaching.

The school acquired its first wireless set in October 1947, and in the same year it was agreed that the School House should be fitted with a bathroom. Also that year, the Education Office advised the managers that the cleaner's wages would be increased from £30 to £36 per annum; inflation had further increased these wages to £45 by January 1949, a 50% increase in under two years.

The Youth Club Drama Group, c.1953.
Back row: Mr Darling – area youth organiser, Rupert Duester, Peter Joy, Stan Dewar, Frank Maries – youth leader. *Front row:* Ivy Rachael, Janet Pratley, Celia Smith, Ray Surch, Peter Walker, Mervyn Bartlett

In September 1948, a parcel containing 70 tins of food arrived from The Mokaka Maori School in New Zealand. Lots were drawn and each child took a gift home. Some items of food were still rationed at this time, so this gift was much appreciated by everyone.

Building improvements included the installation of 'flush lavatories to replace the existing pits' in March 1949, 'a wall to separate the boys and girls yards at the top end', and the fitting of classroom screen doors to divide the main schoolroom so that three classes could be taught separately. The only wash basins were two 'lead lined troughs', and these were replaced. The playground surface was condemned as 'rough and dangerous' by HM Inspectors in their report of July 1950; they recommended that it be 'resurfaced and enlarged to make it suitable for physical exercises'. Several nasty accidents are recorded in the log book, due to falls caused by the rough surface. For a while, The Lamb Inn car park was used for periods of physical training.

In their report of 1950, the Inspectors commented that 'puppetry, dramatisation and art are successfully taught and are sources of enjoyment to the [Junior] pupils'. Needlework was continuing, although it suffered from the lack of a sewing machine, but 'there is no instruction in either housecraft or handicraft'. They also observed that 'teaching methods [in Class 1] are not developing sufficient enterprise and initiative in the children'. On a positive note, they commented that 'the general tone of the school and the good manners and behaviour of the children reflect much credit on the training'. They were impressed by the 'useful work being done to interest parents in the activities of the school', and they noted that a 'flourishing Parent-Teacher Association has been formed'.[126]

Good use continued to be made of the school by other groups within the village. The Youth Club met in the schoolroom each week, and a Drama Group was formed as part of the Youth Club. Amongst former pupils who played an active part in the Drama Group at this time were Rupert Duester, Marjorie Mills and Phil Pratley. The group had several successes at the Cotswold Youth Drama Festival during the mid-1950s; not only was their presentation of *The Sentence* judged to be the best of the festival, but they were also awarded the Progressive Youth Drama Trophy two years in succession.

Medical matters of interest included regular visits by an orthopaedic sister who 'gave foot exercises' to various children, and a dental inspection in 1950 that lasted for three days because of the numbers of children treated on the spot in one of the classrooms. A treadle drill was still used when fillings were necessary. Two years later, the dental visit lasted four days and involved the use of a mobile van parked in The Lamb Inn car park. The case of a twelve year old boy who swallowed a pin is also recorded in the log book. The advice of the RAF Medical Officer was sought and he suggested 'that a cotton wool sandwich should be given'. This was duly administered and the boy was then sent home; the treatment appears to have worked, because he returned to school the next day with a satisfactory report from the MO, much to the relief of the headteacher!

Some threats to health were still serious in the decade after the war. A pupil at the school, Anne Cartlidge, contracted polio and her treatment involved the use of an iron lung. Sadly, she died on the 4th May 1953 at the age of eleven. She is buried in Great Rissington churchyard, and the inscription on her grave includes these lines:

> 'Jesus took a child
> and set her by him'.

A Separate RAF School

As numbers increased, so the problem of overcrowding became more acute. By June 1949, there were 90 children on the register, 45 of whom were from the village and the other 45 were from RAF Little Rissington. There were not enough desks and some of the children had to make do with dining tables. It was very difficult to get supply teachers at this time and there were real problems if one of the two teachers were ill. Miss Sayers, assistant teacher, struggled with 40 infant children aged 4 to 6, whilst Florence Joynes had to take Classes 1 and 2 together with children ranging in age from seven to fourteen. There were complaints from the parents of RAF children, who now began to petition for their own school at the base.

The teaching situation was eased in September 1949 by the appointment of Mr Pizzey as assistant master, but this did not prevent further complaints by the RAF about the 'educational facilities of the school'. The temporary use of the Reading Room at the other end of the village was considered as an extra classroom, but this does not appear to have been pursued. At the beginning of 1952, there were 102 children on the register organised in three classes. In May 1952, seventeen children over the age of eleven were transferred to Bourton County Council School, leaving 78 pupils at Great Rissington. Relief was

From the left: Mrs Kay Lewis; Bryn Lewis, headteacher; Mrs F. Walker, infant teacher, 1954/55.

temporary however, as the numbers were back up to 90 in September (54 RAF children and 36 from the village).

By September 1953, Bryn Lewis had succeeded Florence Joynes as headteacher; he was assisted by Mr Pizzey in Class 2 and Mrs Walker as infant teacher, together with two part-time supervisory assistants, Mrs Sambell and Mrs Pill, and a cook, canteen assistant and a clerical assistant. In addition, Mrs Kay Lewis taught needlework part-time, but she took over the full-time teaching of Class 2 when Mr Pizzey left. The staff were soon overstretched and the problems of overcrowding were now acute; when the school re-opened after Christmas, the numbers on the roll were back up to 104, and reached 115 in July 1954. The headteacher wrote in the log book: 'only absentees make the situation even tolerable at the moment'.

By now, the managers had been advised of the proposal for a school at the RAF base. In February 1954, they passed the following resolution: 'the managers of this school feel very strongly that the provision of a separate school at the RAF station is not in the best interests of the children residing in the area'. In reply, the LEA gave the following reasons for their decision to establish a new school:[127]

> 1) they were acting on the recommendation of HM Inspector of Schools
> 2) there would be a saving on the high cost of transport
> 3) it would be difficult to provide an extension to the existing school buildings.

In May 1955 the RAF Central Flying School carried out a night flying exercise from 9.30 p.m. to 4.30 a.m., involving continuous 'circuits and bumps' with aircraft taking off every 15 to 30 seconds. After a sleepless night of 'sheer torture', Mr Lewis was hardly in a mood to teach the next day. The issue of daytime aircraft noise was to prove to be a very real threat to the future of Great Rissington School.

Mrs Walker with the infant class, 1954/55.

In September 1955, Mr Lewis was advised that a new school on the base at Little Rissington would open in the New Year 1956, and that he was to be appointed headmaster. The RAF School duly opened on time, and Mr Lewis resigned to take up his new appointment in January. Redundancies followed at Great Rissington, as only 34 children remained. By contrast, the RAF School prospered, and by July 1958 there were 99 children on its roll; the Rev. Harry Cheales and Donald Sweeting from Little Rissington were appointed to its management committee.

The Threat of Closure

On 15th June 1955, two HMIs visited the school. The following entry is recorded in the log book:
'General satisfaction was expressed and useful criticism made. Mr Auty was appalled by the noise of the aircraft. He noted that the school was in a direct line with and close to the end of the runway. He further observed the possibility of the school being the scene of a flying accident, and said, "the matter cannot be ignored – must one wait for something to happen before taking action".'

The Primary Education Sub-Committee for Gloucestershire discussed this matter in July, and agreed 'that in view of the noise and possible danger and psychological effect upon the children resulting from the operation of jet aircraft over the premises of this school, a proposal to close the school should be submitted when the Bourton-on-the-Water Secondary Modern School is opened'. Because the RAF Station was a flying

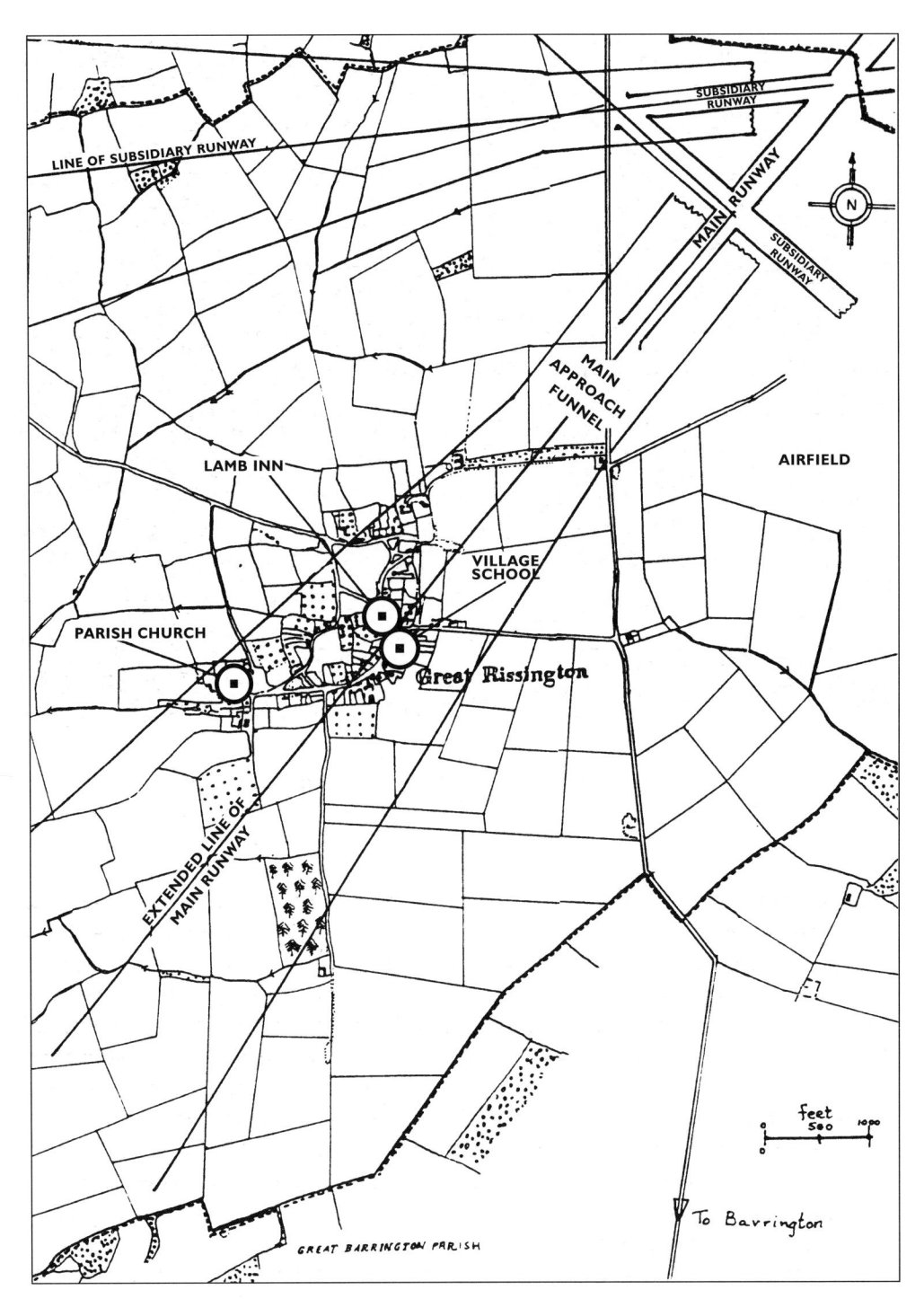

Great Rissington in the 1950s, showing the main approach funnel to RAF Little Rissington. The centre line extending from the main runway is almost directly above the school. Drawn by Norman Good from a contemporary OS map, with reference to an Air Ministry map – *PRO ED 161/5659*.

The school choir, c.1956
Standing: Doreen Webb, Derek Francis, Emlyn Jones – acting headteacher, Brian Agg, David Eeles. *Sitting:* Wendy Chapman, Sheila Brain, Bridget Quinn, Jennifer Jones and her sister, Jean Pratley

training school, it was noted in a letter to the Ministry of Education that a 'considerable amount of take-off and landing procedure is practised'. A further note on file stated that 'some part of an aircraft fell on to the roof some time ago but did not cause any damage'.[128]

It is interesting to note that the County's Development Plan for primary education at that time made provision for the closure of some 203 of the smaller primary schools, and it was hoped that no primary school should have less than 45 pupils, organised in three classes. It is perhaps curious therefore, that the reasons given for the proposed closure of the school made no mention of its size at any point during this controversy.

The school managers were informed of the proposed closure to take effect when the new secondary school in Bourton was completed. They were strongly opposed to closing the school and a petition was hastily organised around the village. The petition, signed by 107 village residents, was forwarded to the Education Committee in February 1956. No further action was taken for almost two years and despite their intention to proceed with the closure, the Committee did not issue a formal notice to that effect.

During the campaign against the proposed closure, a delegation from the village led by Mr H.G. Hughes met officials from the Air Ministry. Their aim was to persuade the RAF to find ways to reduce both the noise and frequency of flights at the Central Flying School.

Mrs Walker with some of the chidren outside the church at Harvest Festival, c.1956.

The delegation proposed that the main runway be realigned so that the constant noise from take-offs and landings would be lessened, but this was rejected as prohibitively expensive. The delegation faced a dilemma; the more they stressed the degree of nuisance to villagers caused by excessive noise and frequency of flights, the greater was the strength of argument in favour of closing the school on these very grounds. The Air Ministry advised the delegation that it was unlikely that the airfield would be needed for flying training *for longer than a further seven years*![129]

Meanwhile, the work of the school continued as normally as possible under the temporary leadership of Emlyn Jones. In spite of the upheaval and uncertainty, four more pupils passed their exams to win places at Westwood's Grammar School.

When it seemed likely that a closure notice would finally be issued, the managers wrote again to the Education Committee opposing the closure of Great Rissington School, which would be 'detrimental to the interests of the children and the general welfare of the village, and such closure will be strongly opposed by the parishioners'. They further wrote that Mr Jones, the supply headteacher, had given an assurance that 'the danger from noise and possible psychological effect or nuisance value of the operation of jet aircraft is practically negligible'.[130]

In the end, the Education Committee decided in March 1958 'not to accelerate the Development Plan proposal for the school which means, of course, that it will remain open for many years so far as anyone is able to say at present'. Now that this uncertainty had been removed, the Committee agreed that 'consideration will be given to the question of staffing'.

XIII

HIGHLIGHTS FROM THE YEARS AFTER 1958

In January 1959, Mrs E.W. Gwynne commenced her appointment as headteacher, a post she was to hold for some 24 years, longer than any other head in the history of the school. Apart from some brief appointments during the 1920s, she was the first married woman to run the school for almost a hundred years. She was ably assisted by Mrs Walker, who was by now the only other permanent teacher on the staff. The school was thus organised into two classes.

School hours were altered in February 1959 to comply with the requirements of the County Education Committee, and to fit in with the bus service, as follows:

> 9.15 a.m. – 12.15 p.m.
> 1.15 p.m. – 3.15 p.m. for infants
> 1.15 p.m. – 3.45 p.m. for junior children

Numbers at the school continued to be dependent on the RAF for several years. Soon after Mrs Gwynne started, the numbers on the roll were 32, but by June they had risen to 55 because the RAF School was full. In September 1959, numbers were back down to 37 as many of the RAF children had transferred to the RAF school. However, as that school once again reached its capacity, additional RAF children were admitted to Great Rissington and so the roll rose steadily, to reach 55 by the following February. Planning classwork through the age ranges must have been extremely difficult in these circumstances; children were transferred temporarily out of the infant class, which had now grown to 33.

The last rector to be chairman of the managers of the school was the Rev. E. Spencer Jones, who resigned in 1959. For more than 115 years the rector of the parish had been either the sole manager or the chairman of the managers of this village school. He was succeeded by Walter Duester, who served as a manager for 25 years and as chairman for thirteen years. By now, the Manor had been bought by the Godmans who remained in the village for some thirty years. They opened up the long room at the Manor to villagers for bingo and whist drives, and children from the school were entertained to tea from time to time.

HM Inspectors visited the school in January 1961, and their report acknowledged the difficulties caused by 'the vicissitudes of the past few years'. They observed a very wide range of attainment among the nineteen junior children, all but one of whom could read.

Many of the children were thought to have few 'out-of-school experiences' but new interests were being fostered through the broadening of the curriculum. Much of the written work was described as meagre in content due to a lack of wide reading, so pupils were being encouraged by the headteacher to borrow county library books. The infants were enjoying a pleasant though limited programme of work.[131]

By October 1961, almost all the RAF children had been withdrawn from Great Rissington following the cancellation of their school bus service. There were now 33 children on the school roll, but without support from RAF families, the number had dwindled to just 27 by May 1962.

The hard winter of 1963 caused problems in the school and the coal stoves proved quite inadequate for the severe conditions. Heavy snow fell during the Christmas holidays, but a path was cut through to the door and the school opened as normal with only three children absent. On January 22nd, outside temperatures fell to 14°F., and inside the classroom 'ink was frozen solid in spite of making [the] stove as hot as possible'. Next day, the temperature in the classroom was still below freezing until 10.30 a.m. Deep snowdrifts made travel difficult, but the school remained open. This combination of snow and sub-zero temperatures continued until the second week of March. A timely addition to the schedule of improvements for the school in 1963 was the provision of a hot water supply.

The school continued to depend on its two coal-burning stoves for heat, and it was sometimes necessary to light the stoves in May or September. At the end of May 1965, both fires had to be lit because the temperature was only 52°F. The situation improved in July 1966, when background electric heaters were installed in the large classroom, but the coal stoves continued in use as the main source of heat until 1972, when they were finally replaced by night storage heaters. Other building work included a new sanitary block and the installation of a telephone for the first time, both in 1968.

If the cook were absent for more than a couple of days meals were usually supplied from Bourton. Sometimes Mrs Sambell would take over at short notice and cook for up to 45 children and staff. Numbers at the school fluctuated between 30 and 40 throughout the 1960s and into the early 1970s, but rose briefly to 46 in 1973 until several RAF children left. About half the children came from Great Rissington, with the others coming from the Camp and surrounding villages.

In April 1966 the BBC contacted Mrs Gwynne to ask if they could film the school and the children for an episode of *Softly, Softly*. Permission was obtained from Shire Hall, but the RAF said that their planes would be flying over the village throughout the day in question and they refused to alter or defer their plans. Much to the disappointment of the children, the BBC then hastily arranged to film at Naunton School, but at the last minute the older children were invited to take part in the filming.

There was much sadness when the rector, William Bates, was killed in a car accident in March 1968. Mr Bates had been a manager of the school for eight years and had visited the school frequently. The school was closed for the afternoon of his funeral to enable the staff and many of the pupils to attend.

In June 1969, the Queen visited RAF Little Rissington and all the children lined the route to wave to her. This barely rated a mention in the log book, but a month later, on

21st July, Mrs Gwynne wrote: 'Moon shot successful. Men walked on the moon for the first time. Children very interested'.

The strikes of 1972 lead to rota power cuts across the whole country. On 17th February, the scheduled power cuts at the school were from 9 a.m. to noon, 3 p.m. to 6 p.m. and 9 p.m. to midnight. The following day, the school closed for an extended half-term break of one week; the normal length of the February half-term holiday at that time was just two days.

John Hughes, a respected farmer in the village, took over as chairman of the managers in June 1973. He served as a manager for 25 years and as chairman for 19 years. By the time he retired in 1992, to be succeeded as chairman of governors by Rupert Duester, the role had changed considerably and much more responsibility had been devolved to governing bodies.

By November 1975, the number of children at the school had fallen to just thirteen, but rose to nineteen by the following April. A few of the parents in the village may have looked to other village schools for their children's education at this time. When the Irish Rangers were posted to the camp at Little Rissington in 1976, numbers increased again, reaching 33 by January 1978. The regiment transferred to Berlin in June 1979, when all remaining children from the Camp left the school.

A new infant teacher, Pauline Greenough, joined the staff in January 1977, and the following year Jane Hemmings started her long association with the school by teaching for two mornings a week. Although Mrs Greenough was not at the school for many years, she was loved by all the children and is remembered by parents and colleagues as an excellent teacher. Whilst on holiday in August 1981, she was knocked down by a charging ewe and sustained a badly broken thigh. She never returned to school, and left the area when her husband moved to a new job.

To celebrate the Queen's Jubilee in June 1977, the children joined a fancy dress parade around the village led by a pipe band. This was followed by a Jubilee party for the children in the school, which was also the venue later in the week for a Jubilee disco for adults. Everyone thoroughly enjoyed themselves amidst a festive mood of national celebration.

The flourishing Parent-Teacher Association of 1950 had long since lapsed, but in 1980 a new group, the Friends of Great Rissington School, was formed. Mrs Gwynne had wisely agreed to its formation so long as it was not called a PTA! The Friends exist to raise funds for the school and to arrange social functions, and to date, many thousands of pounds have been raised to supplement school funds. A wide range of activities have been organised over the years, from pig and ox roasts to punting on the river at Oxford. The Friends have done much to encourage a sense of community amongst all those associated with the school.

The new year of 1982 brought with it heavy snow followed by extremely cold weather; a temperature of minus 21°C was recorded at the school on the night of 13th January. No meals reached the school from Bourton for several days and children had to bring sandwiches. During breaks, the children and staff built igloos in the playground over several days.

A New Headteacher

In July 1982, Mrs Eve Gwynne retired after 24 years as headteacher. She is remembered as a person with a strong presence, who knew what she wanted, and who used tried and tested methods of teaching which may not always have stretched the children to their full potential. Nevertheless, a number of her pupils won places at Westwood's Grammar School. She managed the school over a long period of gradual change, but by the time she retired her health had begun to deteriorate. Mrs Gwynne was succeeded by Mrs Doreen Clegg, previously headteacher at Great Barrington School which had just been closed after a long struggle to remain open. Also from Great Barrington came Ruth Dawson as assistant teacher and Ruby Young as cook.

One of Mrs Clegg's first actions was to reopen the kitchen and the children enjoyed excellent meals prepared by Mrs Young, a trained cook who also catered for various local functions in the area. Mrs Young would often bring in fresh produce from her own garden. Over the next ten years, however, the LEA gradually reduced and eventually withdrew funding for school meals, and Mrs Young's hours were cut to a level which made it uneconomic for her to continue. Mrs Clegg noted in the log book in 1985 that 'school meals seem to have taken more of my time than anything else'.

Several children from US Airforce families stationed at Little Rissington started at the school in 1983, though most left at the age of six to go to the American School at the Camp. Also that year, Sir Alec Rose came to the school and enthralled the children with his account of his single handed voyage around the world in his yacht, *Lively Lady*.

Computers first appeared in the school during 1984. Initially, a single computer was purchased with help from the Friends, and soon one of the parents, Malcolm Ford was running a computer club in the evenings for interested parents and villagers. The computer age had finally reached the school and a whole new generation of busy parents were expected to learn new skills in support of their children.

Some of the frustrations experienced by a headteacher in keeping a small school running with little external assistance become apparent from entries in the log book and surviving correspondence. Too many small matters took a disproportionate amount of chasing up to resolve. A few examples of day-to-day problems illustrate the varied concerns of the headteacher:

- the telephone did not work for a whole week and the school was without any means of external communication; BT were unable to trace the fault.
- a request for extra electric points badly needed in the teaching areas was eventually turned down some nine months later. Only intervention by the chairman of governors brought about a change of mind.
- there were constant problems after the fitting of a frost thermostat, which actually *prevented* the heating from coming on when needed. SEB denied liability and so contractors had to be brought in from elsewhere, but only after many calls and hours of wasted time. Then the fault occurred again – and again!
- There were endless problems with catering supplies; the same problems kept recurring despite repeated phonecalls and letters. Sometimes there were no

School photo, 1988.
Back row: Rebecca Parkes, Eleanor Mayo, Jonathon Ford, Simon Plater, Jenny Griffiths, Joanne Littrell, Laura Blake, Sam Pennington. *3rd row:* Charles Hayter, Emily Martin, Mervyn Mayo, Leigh Dailey, Sorrel Hunter, Andrew Surch, Simon Collett, Vicky Blake. *2nd row:* James Mollison, Rachel Fain, Kara Filbey, Grace Mayo, Emily Boyes, Lotte Couchman. *Front row:* Rebecca Martin, Kelly Fain, Charlotte Garwood, Ruth Dawson, Kate Bishop, Doreen Clegg, Chris Pescod, Samantha Poverud, Tiffany Hayter, Amey Fagg

deliveries of some items needed for that day's lunch, whilst on other days provisions were left outside the gates of the school long before it opened in the morning. And numerous letters of complaint about the continued supply of unpalatable and expensive pre-prepared potatoes went unheeded.
- Following a break-in at the School House, Mrs Clegg had to drive to Bourton and fetch the local policeman, as he had no transport of his own.
- Several acts of vandalism and threatening behaviour had to be dealt with.

As part of the school's involvement in the wider community, regular fund raising events were arranged. Over a number of years, the children raised many hundreds of pounds for Dr Barnardo's charity. In 1984, a sponsored 'hush' was organised, in which the children succeeded in occupying themselves on various activities in class without saying a word for up to two hours, much to the surprise and delight of the teachers!

The school float with a scene from *Oliver* at the Bourton carnival, 1988. Parents and 'Friends' taking part were: Mike Pennington (top left), Rupert Duester, Janne Bishop, Malcolm Ford, Susie Clark, Betty Duester, Paul Clark.

Harvest suppers became a tradition at the school, and continued until the demise of the kitchen. In 1986, for example, 97 people from the village sat down to enjoy a variety of cold meats and salads, supplemented by jacket potatoes, followed by apple pie and cream. After the meal there was usually some form of amusing light entertainment, involving either the children, the women, or the men of the village. These and other occasions helped to ensure that the school remained at the heart of the village community.

Another tradition which has died out now that there is no longer a school kitchen is the annual Christmas dinner for all the children and parents of those leaving at the end of the year. The food was provided by the staff and supplemented from school funds, and the cook, Mrs Pescod, commented that 'she enjoyed doing some real cooking for a change'.

For much of the 1980s, Great Rissington School participated in the area Music Festival held each year at Bourton Vale School. Musical productions were coordinated by the county music adviser, who worked with the children in each of the participating local schools. The schools were only brought together for a couple of rehearsals before the full performance, to which parents and the public were invited.

In 1988, the juniors completed a religious education project to produce their own newspaper, *The Bethlehem News*. With the help of the Rev. David Bush, the children imagined themselves to be reporters at the scene of the first Christmas. They visited the Bailey Litho printing works in Dursley to watch their paper being 'put to bed', and then returned to school with their own copies 'hot off the press'. Later that year, Flora Meredith won a county-wide competition to prepare a page for a calendar to be produced for the Stroud Meningitis Trust, winning £225 for the school. And in July, the school float organised by the Friends and featuring a scene from *Oliver* won first place in the Bourton carnival. By the end of a successful year, the number of children had risen to 35.

In common with many other villages, there were by now increasing numbers of people living in Great Rissington because it was a pleasant place to live, but who commuted to work elsewhere. It is perhaps a measure of the success of the school that it has succeeded in attracting not only children from long-established village families, but also those from families employed in business and 'professional' occupations.

The daily routine of life at school was interrupted in May 1990 by the arrival of an unwanted swarm of bees, which decided that the disused chimney would make a comfortable new home. Some of the bees found their way down the chimney and into the classroom. One of the local beekeepers, Ray Surch, was summoned and came to smoke them out after the children had gone home for the day. As the chimney was blocked by soot and debris, more smoke ended up in the classroom than up the chimney. The next day the pest exterminator arrived and proceeded to put a smoke pellet in the chimney, but once again the classroom filled up with smoke. He then sprayed the outside of the chimney, with the result that stunned and dying bees ended up in the classroom and all around the entrance door. Meanwhile, the children were singing hymns in the playground as part of the Wednesday assembly, led by the local Catholic priest. They were sent home early that day.

Arrangements were made for the chimney to be swept during the half term break several days later. Two men came, equipped only with a brush and rods. The result of their attempts to 'sweep' a partly blocked chimney was that the classroom was caked in soot, requiring contract cleaners to clear up the mess on the Saturday. They warned that the soot would settle again, and staff and children had to spend the following Monday cleaning up books and other apparatus. By then, the novelty of this little diversion had worn off and the children were probably glad to get back to their lessons.

During the Gulf War, the school's long association with the base at RAF Little Rissington was renewed. The base itself housed the 870th USAF Contingency Hospital, which was activated to receive any US casualties from Operation Desert Storm. Considerable numbers of American medical personnel were stationed at the base for the period of the Gulf emergency, and local people were asked to make their stay as comfortable as possible. The whole school participated in making an enormous collage to decorate a recreation room at the base. Each child made a picture of him or herself, dressed it and stuck it on to the collage, which was then carefully taken up to the base, unrolled and hung up. After the war, the Americans presented the school with a Certificate of Appreciation.

A new mezzanine floor was built in the junior classroom during the summer of 1992, greatly extending the usable space for the children. This would not have been possible but for the considerable input of funds raised by the Friends of the School, and the professional help given by some of the parents, together with assistance in carrying out much of the preparatory work, cleaning and painting.

By now, the kitchen had been condemned as unhygienic and meals were being delivered to the school in containers by an external contractor. The provision of cooked meals had become uneconomic following the LEA decision to withdraw its subsidy, and as the quality of the meals was unsatisfactory, more and more children were opting to bring in a packed lunch. After well over a year of constant problems relating to the school meals service, the kitchen was finally closed amidst considerable controversy early in 1993. The kitchen was subsequently converted into a very pleasant Activity Room for music, painting and craft work, group projects, and simple cookery. Staff were also able to use the room for meetings and breaks.

The school has no sports field of its own, but has been able to make use of the village sports field nearby since 1965. The boys play football during the autumn and spring terms, and in recent years they have been coached by parents, first by Rob Gorton and later by Geoff Close. Under their guidance the boys have had success in matches against other schools and were unbeaten for three years from 1992. During the summer term, both the girls and boys play cricket and rounders, again with some help from parents. Mrs Dawson takes the children for athletics during the summer and the girls for netball or the occasional game of 'unihoc' in winter. Until recently, parents have also assisted with swimming at The Lamb Inn pool, but since that closed, swimming instruction has been provided at the Cotswold Leisure Centre in Cirencester. There have also been occasions in the recent past when tennis coaching and rugby lessons were available for the older boys and girls.

In a small village school, the participation of parents helps to widen the choice of activities available to children. Parents at Great Rissington School have contributed in many areas of the curriculum, including the provision of recorder lessons and a French club.

A Time of Change

During the 1980s, a number of Government education initiatives had placed increasing demands on teachers and given additional responsibilities to governors. Much greater emphasis was placed on the curriculum, with its four fundamental principles: breadth, balance, relevance and differentiation. A definition of the curriculum declared that it includes:

> 'not only the formal programme of lessons, but also the informal programmes of so-called extra-curricular activities as well as all those features which produce the school's 'ethos', such as the quality of relationships, the concern for equality of opportunity, the values exemplified in the way the school sets about its task and the way in which it is organised and managed.'[132]

This process of change was underlined by *The Education Reform Act* of 1988, which made provision for a national curriculum consisting of core subjects – maths, English and science – and a number of foundation subjects, together with religious education.

An example of parental involvement; Philippa Duckmanton teaches the recorder to Matthew Gilbert, Holly Trigg and Toby Clark. *Photo courtesy The Journal Series, Evesham.*

Nationally prescribed tests were to be introduced for children aged 7, 11, 14, and 16, and Local Management of Schools was to be phased in, by which local authorities handed over responsibility for school budgets to governing bodies. Amongst other provisions of the Act, school governing bodies were given powers, if certain conditions were met, to opt out of local authority control.

It is beyond the scope of this book to examine the merits of these various measures and subsequent changes to the national curriculum, except to say that they have imposed an enormous additional burden on the teaching staff of a small primary school. New policies and schemes of work have been required, which need to be updated every time a change is announced at national level. A comprehensive School Development Plan has had to be drawn up covering every aspect of school life, including its relationship with the local community. These requirements have resulted in the need to adopt a much more professional approach to the management of schools; headteachers and governing bodies are now much more accountable for adopting sound policies and procedures than hitherto, all of which are subject to close scrutiny at the time of an OFSTED[133] inspection.

The preparation of a draft School Development Plan began towards the end of 1993, but was put on hold because of the impending retirement of the headteacher, Mrs Doreen Clegg. In almost twelve years as head, Mrs Clegg had seen the numbers at the school rise steadily, a reflection of its growing reputation as a happy and successful village school, where children of all abilities received a sound education within a caring environment. She left the school financially well placed to cope with the many changes now required in planning for the future. Mrs Dawson took over as acting headteacher for the summer term of 1994.

The present headteacher, Mrs Elizabeth Franklin, took up her appointment in September 1994. By then, the number of children at the school had risen to 52, organised into three classes. In her first address to parents in October, Mrs Franklin said: "We are very fortunate in being able to work and learn in this beautiful village in a lovely natural environment. The school is a central focal point in a village community and I want to build upon the existing links with the community." Amongst other things, Mrs Franklin also commented on the positive links that already existed with the Church.

It was not long before the children were involved in collecting a total of 76 boxes of toys to be sent to Bosnia and Croatia in time for Christmas. And to help foster a sense of caring for people in the local community, the older children visited Salmondsbury House in Bourton-on-the-Water with Christmas gifts and cards. They also entertained the residents with songs they had learnt for the Christmas play. The visit was much appreciated and was the first of many.

To cope with the actual and anticipated growth in numbers, the governors had endorsed the appointment of an additional part-time teacher for the Reception Class, Anne Adams. This post was initially financed from reserves. There were further changes in teaching staff a year later when Diane White resigned and went with her husband to live in Vietnam. She has returned several times and talked to the children about life in a Buddhist country, bringing with her a selection of Vietnamese musical instruments, hats, silks, incense sticks and food.

One of the first priorities for Mrs Franklin was to draw up a School Development Plan. This was completed in stages and subsequently approved by the governors. The Plan established priorities for the next four years and set out a timetable of actions covering every aspect of the school, including the updating and development of a whole range of written policies and procedures. By the end of 1996, much of this additional work had been completed by Mrs Franklin and the teaching staff; many policies were drawn up and agreed, including among others, those for each of the core subjects in the curriculum, special educational needs, pay, equality of opportunity, worship, religious education, homework, display, and behaviour. These and other policies, together with a new prospectus, set out clearly the school's aims and values.

1996 was an important year in the history of the school. A major building programme was completed with funding from the LEA and generous additional help from several anonymous donors. Not only was a well-equipped classroom added to the back of the school, but also the interior of the existing building was transformed by the addition of a second floor. This created a further classroom and office upstairs and released space downstairs for a permanent hall to be used for assemblies, physical education, music, and school plays. In its centenary year, this late Victorian school building now provides a modern purpose-built environment inside, while retaining its familiar and attractive exterior. The transformation has been completed with the addition of a new piano, up-to-date computers, audio and PE equipment, and a mobile stage.

In December, the new hall was the venue for the Christmas production of *Where Will He Be Born?*, largely written and adapted by Mrs Franklin. This was an imaginative and highly successful nativity play involving all 69 children in the school in scenes from around the world. The children sang some sixteen songs from memory and seemed to enjoy

The present headteacher, Elizabeth Franklin, with Luke Rix and Caroline Harington, 1995.

Great Rissington School, winter 1995.

themselves in their colourful costumes. Three performances were given on consecutive days and £176 was collected and donated to the NSPCC.

The early months of 1997 were especially busy for the teaching staff as final preparations were made for the OFSTED inspection over three days in April. A great deal had already been achieved and the governors were confident that this modern, happy and successful village school would receive a favourable inspection report. The teachers found the presence of inspectors in class over the three days to be highly stressful, but were delighted that the inspection had gone well. As this book goes to press, the governors have received a verbal report from the inspectors which commends the school highly, both for the quality of teaching and learning and for the relationships between staff and pupils and between parents and staff. No key issues for action were identified that were not already being addressed, which is a great tribute to the hard work and dedication of all the staff. The following is a summary of the main strengths of the school as identified by the inspectors:

- excellent leadership, management and efficiency
- the school provides its pupils with a good education
- the quality of teaching is sound overall and much of it is good
- there is good provision for spiritual, moral, social and cultural development
- there is a caring atmosphere in the school and relationships are very good
- work is meticulously planned and matched to the individual needs of the children
- accommodation and learning resources are of good quality
- the governors take an active part in the school and its development
- the school is a happy community with a positive ethos and very supportive parents
- the behaviour of the children is generally good and they are interested in their work

The report concludes that this village school offers 'very good value for [public] money'. Summing up, Inspector Ralph Griffin said that "this is one of the best schools I have inspected. Your biggest task now is to maintain what you have already achieved".

Much has changed since the school was rebuilt on a new site one hundred years ago. The days when only the children of tradesmen and agricultural workers in the village attended the school have gone, though this was still very much the pattern until the coming of the RAF and the Second World War. With the decline in agricultural employment and the widespread ownership of motor cars has come an enormous increase in both social and geographical mobility and the consequent break-up of relatively stable village communities. Now, the children of parents in business and the professions who have moved into the village but work elsewhere attend the school alongside those of families who have lived in the village for generations. This diversity has helped the school to survive and grow in recent years. After successfully overcoming threats of closure, the school is well placed to thrive long into the next century and to remain very much at the heart of this rural village community.

APPENDIX 1

The Standards of Examination laid down in the Codes of the Education Department, (1890) [1]

Standard 1 (seven years of age)
  Reading - Read a short paragraph from a book, mostly in monosyllables.
  Writing - Write on a blackboard or slate, from dictation, ten easy words commencing with capital letters.
  Arithmetic - Numbers up to 1000. Simple addition and subtraction of 3 figure numbers. The multiplication table to 6 times 12.
  English - Repeat twenty lines of simple verse.
  Geography - Explain a plan of the school and playground. The four cardinal points. The meaning and use of a map.

Standard 2 (eight years of age)
  Reading - Read a short paragraph from an elementary reading book.
  Writing - A passage of 6 lines from the same reading book, slowly read once and then dictated.
  Arithmetic - Numbers up to 100,000. The 4 simple rules to short division. The multiplication table and pence table to12s.
  English - Repeat 40 lines of poetry and know their meaning. Point out nouns/verbs
  Geography - The size and shape of the world. Geographical terms simply explained and illustrated by reference to a map of England. Physical geography of hills and rivers.

Standard 3 (nine years of age)
  Reading - Read a passage from a more advanced reading book or from stories of English history.
  Writing - Six lines from one of the reading books, slowly read once and then dictated.
  Arithmetic - The rules for long division. Addition and subtraction of money.
  English - Recite with intelligence and expression 60 lines of poetry, and know their meaning. Point out nouns, verbs, adjectives and personal pronouns and form simple sentences containing them.
  Geography - Physical and political geography of England, with special knowledge of the district in which the school is situated.

Standard 4 (ten years of age)
  Reading - Read a few lines from a reading book or history of England.
  Writing - Eight lines of poetry or prose, slowly read once and then dictated.
  Arithmetic - Compound rules (money) and reduction of common weights and measures.
  English - Recite 80 lines of poetry and explain the words and allusions. Parse easy sentences, and show by examples the use of each of the parts of speech.
  Geography - Physical and political geography of the British Isles, British North America and Australia, with knowledge of their productions.

Standard 5 (eleven years of age)
Reading - Read a passage from some standard author, or from a history of England.
Writing - Write from memory the substance of a short story read out twice; spelling, handwriting and correct expression to be considered.
Arithmetic - Addition and subtraction of proper fractions, with denominations not exceeding 10. Practice, bills of parcels, and single rule of three by the method of unity.
English - Recite 100 lines from a standard poet and explain the words and allusions. Parse and analyse simple sentences, and know the method of forming English nouns, adjectives and verbs from each other.
Geography - Geography of Europe, physical and political. Latitude and longitude. Day and night. The seasons.

Standard 6 (twelve years of age)
Reading - Read a passage from one of Shakespeare's historical plays, or from some other standard author or from a history of England.
Writing - A short theme or letter on an easy subject; spelling, handwriting and composition to be considered.
Arithmetic - Fractions, vulgar and decimal; simple proportion and simple interest.
English - Recite 150 lines from Shakespeare or Milton, or some other standard author, and explain the words and allusions. Parse and analyse a short complex sentence, and know the meaning and use of Latin prefixes in the formation of English words.
Geography - Geography of the world generally, and especially the British Colonies. Trade. Circumstances which determine climate.

Standard 7 - Introduced in 1882 - (thirteen years of age)
Reading - Read a passage from Shakespeare or Milton or other standard author, or from a history of England.
Writing - A theme or letter; composition, spelling and handwriting to be considered.
Arithmetic - Compound proportion, averages and percentages.
English - Recite 150 lines from Shakespeare or Milton or other standard author, and explain the words and allusions. Analyse sentences and know prefixes and terminations generally.
Geography - The ocean. Currents and tides. General arrangement of the planetary system. The phases of the moon.

Very few rural children ever reached Standard 7.

Explanatory notes in the *Cyclopaedia of Education* state that the age given for each standard 'denotes the age at which that standard should be passed by the average scholar who passed Standard 1 at seven years of age'. However, 'owing to past neglect, indifference ... and ineffective operation of the law of compulsory school attendance over large areas of the country, children of much older years are to be found in each standard.'[2] Right up to the First World War, many children left school never having progressed beyond Standard 4.

APPENDIX 2

The Relative Value of Money and Inflation

There is no easy way to compare how much things cost or what they were worth from one period to another. There is no single multiplier that can be applied to a sum of money in the past to convert it to a present day equivalent, because there are too many variables. For example, money wages and incomes have altered quite differently for people in different occupations. Prices paid for different items have not moved in a uniform way over time, so that changes in income may not represent similar changes in standards of living. Wages and prices have varied quite widely over time in different parts of the country. And rising living standards and advances in technology have given rise to significant changes in consumer spending patterns; for example, the percentage of income spent by a labourer on bread or food a hundred years ago will be very different today.

In an attempt to overcome these difficulties, economists have developed cost-of-living indices to facilitate comparisons in the value of money, and indices of wage rates and earnings to calculate changes in the amount of money available to different occupations or social groups. These allow approximate comparisons to be made about the value of things in the past which have a general significance, but they may be misleading if applied to a particular sum of money at a particular time, and it is important to know how the relative weighting of differernt items in an index have changed over time. To make matters more difficult, several people using different assumptions have calculated different indices, making comparisons still more difficult.

With these problems in mind, Charles Feinstein calculated new indices for cost of living and nominal wages. For the purposes of this book, a few examples will suffice:[3]

(1913=100)

Year	Nominal earnings	Cost of living	Real earnings
1840	43	105	41
1873	75	111	67
1896	79	85	93
1913	100	100	100
1918	211	202	104
1932	189	142	133
1948	456	270	169
1960	949	429	221
1979	6236	1946	320
1990	17574	4329	406

APPENDIX 3

School and Village Numbers

Number of Children on the Register and Average Attendance (where known)[4]

Year	No. on Register	Average Attendance	Year	No. on Register	Average Attendance
1846	39	-	1921	41	39
1871	-	56	1922	33	31
1885	-	70	1923	30	29
1897	-	75	1924	31	29
1900	85	72	1925	27	26
1901	91	75	1926	29	27
1902	80	76	1927	28	26
1903	85	77	1928	31	29
1904	78	75	1929	34	30
1905	75	72	1930	33	32
1906	73	71	1931	42	40
1907	78	75	1932	45	40
1908	84	76	1933	49	45
1909	82	71	1934	46	43
1910	74	61	1935	43	41
1911	70	60	1936	43	41
1912	67	63	1937	42	38
1913	76	69	1938	41	38
1914	70	65	1939	71	56
1915	66	62	1941	54	48
1916	-	64	1947	66	-
1917	-	54	1949	90	-
1918	-	47	1952	102 (Jan.)	-
1919	-	46	1954	115 (July)	-
1920	45	41	1955	34 (Sept.)	-

Numbers on the Register after 1955

Year	Month	Number	Year	Month	Number
1959	Mar	32	1980	Sept	24
1959	June	55	1982	Sept	24
1961	Mar	41	1984	Sept	25
1963	Mar	29	1986	Sept	23
1965	Mar	35	1988	Sept	35
1970	Apr	37	1990	Sept	32
1973	Sept	39	1992	Sept	45
1974	Sept	23	1994	Sept	52
1975	Nov	13	1996	Nov	69
1976	Sept	19		Projected	
1978	Jan	33	1997	Sept	75

Population figures for Great Rissington[5]

1735 1801 1811 1821 1831 1841 1851 1861 1871 1881 1891 1901 1921 1931 1951 1991

240* 349 361 446 468 483 493 499 481 413 419 347 245 265 304 330

*estimated

NOTES

1. Quoted from the Report of the Education Department of the Privy Council, 1895, p. 103
2. This and subsequent extracts from the *Stow Deanery Magazine* 1902-5, GRO, P 317 IN 4/3
3. *Great Rissington 1857-1957*, (Gt. Riss. W.I.), available in the Gloucestershire Collection, Gloucester Library
4. Anthea Jones, *The Cotswolds* (Phillimore, 1994), p. 190
5. *Victoria County History* (VCH), Vol. VI, p. 103
6. *Great Rissington 1857-1957*
7. *VCH* Vol. VI, p.106
8. Select Committee on the Education of the Poor, 1818, Vol. I. Church of England Record Centre
9. Education Enquiry, 1833, Vol. I. Church of England Record Centre
10. Frank Booth, *Robert Raikes of Gloucester* (NCEC, 1980), p. 68
11. A. Platts and G.H. Hainton, *Education in Gloucestershire: A Short History* (G.C.C., 1954), p. 51
12. T.W. Laqueur, *Religion and Respectability* (Yale University Press, 1976), p. 44
13. In 1841, the population of Britain was 18.5m – by 1901, it had risen to 37.5m
14. *Culture and Education in Victorian England*, ed. by Scott and Fletcher (Bucknell University Press, USA, 1990), p. 67
15. The National Society's file on Gt. Rissington School at the Church of England Record Centre
16. PRO, ED 21/5842
17. PRO, ED 21/5842
18. Church of England Record Centre
19. Church of England Record Centre
20. Church of England Record Centre
21. Richard Venwell, a labourer aged 21, sentenced to be transported in 1831. *Transportees from Gloucestershire to Australia 1783-1842*. Glos. Records Series vol.1 (1988) p.12
22. GRO, Gloucestershire Summary Convictions Register, QGc9/2
23. The term 'Code' is the short title for the Code of Regulations by the Lords of the Committee of the Privy Council on Education
24. J. Stuart Maclure, *Educational Documents 1816 to the Present Day* (Methuen, 1973), p. 71
25. Gordon Batho, *Political Issues in Education* (Cassell, 1990), p. 5 (from *Report*, 1861, vol. VII, 1, p. 182)
26. Gillian Sutherland, *Elementary Education in the Nineteenth Century* (Historical Assoc., 1971), p. 12
27 *Cyclopaedia of Education*, 3rd edn. (Sonnenschein, 1892), p. 160
28 J.E. Dunfold, *Her Majesty's Inspectorate of Schools in England and Wales 1860-1870*, Educational Administration & History: Monograph No. 9 (University of Leeds,1980), p. 20
29. GRO, S 269/1/1 – 4th May 1888 and 22nd January 1886 respectively
30. GRO, S 269/1/1
31. GRO; D 1395 1/6 (research by Norman Good)
32. Gt. Ris'n. log book, June 1875: transcribed by Mrs Clare Mayo from the early log books before they were lost
33. Pamela Horn, *The Victorian and Edwardian Schoolchild* (Alan Sutton, 1989), p. 70
34. The Agricultural Children's Education Act
35. GRO, SB 32/1
36. J.S. Maclure, *Educational Documents*, p. 99

37. G.A.N. Lowndes, *The Silent Social Revolution* (Oxford University Press, 1950 edn.), p. 5
38. PRO, ED 7/34
39. *VCH* vol. VI, p. 106
40. *Kelly's Directory*, Gloucestershire 1856
41. This and the HMI reports of 1877 and 1878 transcribed by Mrs Mayo from the school log book
42. Transcribed by Mrs Mayo
43. PRO, ED 2/182
44. PRO, ED 2/182
45. PRO, ED 2/182
46. PRO, ED 21/5842
47. Recalled by Mrs Kay Lewis from the early school log books; also *Great Rissington 1857-1957*
48. *Great Rissington 1857-1957*
49. GRO, S 268/1
50. GRO, SB 32/1 & 32/2
51. J.E. Dunfold, *Her Majesty's Inspectorate of Schools in England and Wales 1860-1870*, p. 50
52. P. Horn, *Labouring Life in the Victorian Countryside* (1995 edn.), p. 49
53. J.E. Dunfold, p. 30-31
54. *Great Rissington 1857-1957*
55. GRO, SB/32/6
56. *The Wilts and Gloucestershire Standard*, Feb. 1897
57. From a list transcribed from the school log book by Mrs Mayo
58. L. Black, *History of Education Society Bulletin* – Number 25, Spring 1980, p. 40
59. *Great Rissington 1857-1957*
60. *Great Rissington News*, June 1987 – article by Mrs Eleanor Ford
61. Transcribed from the log book by Mrs Mayo
62. Transcribed from the log book by Mrs Mayo
63. *Great Rissington 1857-1957*
64. GRO, SB/32/1
65. *The Wilts and Gloucestershire Standard*, 2nd Oct. 1897. This and subsequent extracts on microfilm at the Bingham Library, Cirencester
66. GRO, AE/B/1
67. According to *Great Rissington 1857-1957*, local stone was carted from Hill Quarry by W. Bartlett
68. The edition of Sat. 25th September 1897.
69. *VCH*, vol. VI, p. 99
70. G.E. Mingay, *A Social History of the English Countryside* (Routledge, 1990), p.171
71. The Gloucestershire Collection at Gloucester Library
72. *Great Rissington 1857-1957*
73. GRO, ROL II/4
74. *Great Rissington 1857-1957*
75. *Great Rissington 1857-1957*
76. This and subsequent extracts from *Stow Deanery Magazine* – GRO, P 317 IN 4/3
77. *Stow Deanery Magazine* June 1902, GRO, P 317 IN 4/3
78. Copy of testimonial supplied by Mrs Mary Robbins
79. Transcribed from the log book by Mrs Mayo
80. GRO, K 484/164
81. GRO, K 484/164
82. GRO, K 484/164
83. GRO, K 484/164
84. GRO, K 484/164
85. *Gloucestershire Echo*, April 12th 1939
86. The full title was The School Attendance and Medical Inspection Sub-Committee
87. GRO, CE/M5/1, Minute book May 1903 to Jan. 1906, pp. 75-6
88. GRO, CE/M5/2, Minute book Feb. 1906 – Dec. 1908, p. 444
89. HMSO, 3rd impression, 1927, p. 9
90. GRO, S 268/2
91. S. Gelbier, The First Stirrings of a School Dental Service for London – A Dissertation (1980)
92. Platts and Hainton, *Education in Gloucestershire* p. 92
93. This and subsequent HMI reports to 1910, GRO, K 484/164
94. *History of Education Society Bulletin 27*, Spring 1981 – Robin Betts

95. PRO, ED 21/5842
96. This and subsequent correspondence about the School House – GRO, K 484/164
97. Log book, 1974-93
98. Interview with Maud Pill, Nov. 1996
99. *Great Rissington 1857-1957*; also *Education in Gloucestershire* p. 84
100. F.E. Green, *The Tyranny of the Countryside*, (T. Fisher Unwin – 1913) p. 69
101. Mr Demer remained as Headmaster of Sherborne School for 32 years
102. *The Wilts and Gloucestershire Standard*, July 1916
103. *The Wilts and Gloucestershire Standard*, June & August 1916
104. Great Rissington Church
105. J.S. Maclure, *Educational Documents*, from *Hansard*, August 10th, 1917
106. GRO, S 268/3
107. This and subsequent extracts from HMI reports up to 1932 – PRO, ED 21/28811
108. *Wilts and Gloucestershire Standard*, Jan. 1920
109. *Great Rissington 1857-1957*
110. PRO, ED 21/28811
111. Admission Book, GRO, S 268/1
112. PRO, ED 21/51799 (February 1936)
113. Discussion with Arthur Lane, Kath Ricketts, Kath Shergold and Fred Webb, Jan. 1997
114. *Great Rissington 1857-1957*
115. This and subsequent events for 1935-37, *The Wilts and Gloucestershire Standard*
116. Discussion with Anne Grave (née Duester), Mabel Herbert (née Cambray) and Rupert Duester, Dec.1996
117. GRO, D 3355/42 – The diaries of Canon Grice-Hutchinson, Sept. 9th 1940
118. This and many entries after 1945 (too numerous to list individually) Log book, 1941-74
119. *The Wilts and Gloucestershire Standard*, 13th Feb. 1943
120 GRO, SM 268/M1
121. GRO, D 3355/42 to 47; extracts quoted by kind permission of the Grice-Hutchinson family and the GRO
122. Rest Centres (often in schools) were used as places of temporary shelter for those displaced by air raids
123. Gordon Batho, *Political Issues in Education*, p. 20
124. Platts & Hainton, *Education in Gloucestershire*, p.118
125. PRO, ED 161/5659
126. Log book, 1941-74
127. GRO, SM 268/M1
128. GRO, K 484/164
129. PRO, ED 161/5659
130. GRO, K 484/164
131. Log book, 1941-74
132. *The Curriculum from 5-16*, Her Majesty's Inspectorate of Schools, (HMSO 1985)
133. Office for Standards in Education

Notes to Appendices

1. As set out in the *Cyclopaedia of Education*, 3rd edn. (Sonnenschein, 1892). There were earlier versions of these Standards
2. *Cyclopaedia of Education*, 3rd edn. p. 424
3. L. Munby, *How Much is that Worth?* (Phillimore, 2nd edn. 1996) p. 56, quoted by permission of the Brit. Association for Local History
4. PRO, ED 161/5659, GRO Summary Registers, log books and *Kelly's Directories*
5. *VCH* vols. II and VI; 1991 figure, *Village Appraisal*

BIBLIOGRAPHY

Aldrich, A., *School and Society in Victorian Britain* (College of Preceptors, 1995)
Batho, G., *Political Issues in Education* (Cassell, 1989)
Booth, F., *Robert Raikes of Gloucester* (NCEC, 1980)
Calder, A., *The People's War* (1969 – reprinted by Pimlico, 1992)
Chapman, C.R., *The Growth of British Education and its Records* (Lochin Publishing, 2nd edn. 1992)
Churches and Education, History of Education Society Conference Papers – Dec. 1983
Culture and Education in Victorian England, ed. P. Scott and P. Fletcher (Bucknell Univ. Press, 1990)
Dent, H.C., *The Education Act 1944* (University of London, 1945 edn.)
Dunford, J.E., *Her Majesty's Inspectorate of Schools in England and Wales 1860-1870* (Museum of the History of Education, University of Leeds, 1986)
Green, F.E., *The Tyranny of the Countryside* (Unwin, 1913)
Handbook of Suggestions for Teachers, Board of Education (HMSO, 1927 edn.)
Hardy, S., *The Village School* (Brechinset Publications, 1979)
History of Education Society Bulletins, Nos. 25, 27 and 35
Horn, P., *Labouring Life in the Victorian Countryside* (Alan Sutton, 1995 edn.)
Horn, P., *The Victorian and Edwardian Schoolchild* (Alan Sutton, 1989)
Jones, A., *The Cotswolds* (Phillimore, 1994)
Kay-Shuttleworth, J., *Memorandum on Popular Education* (1868 – reprinted, Woburn Press, 1969)
Maclure, J.S., *Educational Documents* (Methuen, 3rd edn. 1973)
Mingay, G.E., *A Social History of the English Countryside* (Routledge, 1990)
Munby, L., *How Much is that Worth?* (Phillimore, 2nd edn. 1996)
Laqueur, T.W., *Religion and Respectability – Sunday Schools and Working Class Culture 1780-1850* (Yale, 1976)
Lee, L., *Cider with Rosie* (Penguin, 1974 edn.)
Leinster-Mackay, D., *Cross-pollinators of English Education: Case Studies of Three Victorian School Inspectors* (Museum of the History of Education, Leeds, 1986)
Lewis, J.R., *The Village School* (Hale, 1989)
Lowndes, G.A.N., *The Silent Social Revolution* (Oxford, reprinted 1950)
Platts, A. & Hainton, G.H., *Education in Gloucestershire – A Short History* (G.C.C., 1954)
Stephens, W.B. and Unwin, R.W., *Materials for the Local and Regional Study of Schooling 1700-1900* (British Records Association, 1987)
Sutherland, G., *Elementary Education in the Nineteenth Century* (Historical Association, London, 1971)
Victoria County History, Glos. VI (1955)
Victorian Countryside, Vol. 2, ed. G.E. Mingay (Routledge, 1981)
Village Education in Nineteenth-Century Oxfordshire, ed. P. Horn (1979)

Extracts from *How Much is that Worth?*, have been included in this book by kind permission of The British Association for Local History. Copies can be obtained from the Society at: Box 1576, Salisbury, SP2 8SY.

GREAT RISSINGTON